God's Executioner: The Ervil LeBaron Tragedy

God's Executioner: The Ervil LeBaron Tragedy

The Story about the Rise and Fall of Ervil LeBaron

DeWayne C. Hafen

Published by Transition Valley Media

Copyright ©2023 by Dewayne C. Hafen

All Rights Reserved

First Published in 2023 in the United States of America by Transition Valley Media

Print Softcover ISBN 979-8-9895184-0-1

Print Hardcover ISBN 979-8-9895184-2-5

eBook ISBN 979-8-9895184-1-8

Library of Congress Control Number: 2023950420

Printed in the United States

This book is dedicated to all of those who were victims of Ervil and the Lambs of God: Especially those who were unwillingly trapped in familial relations with them and still suffer because of that relationship.

Foreword

I had the opportunity to hear this story many times and every time I suggested that Dewayne Hafen should put the story in book form so that others could learn and avoid future tragedy.

It truly was a tragedy what happened to all the victims of Ervil LeBaron, from those who died at his bidding to his kids and his followers. Ervil and his followers left a path of death and destruction. The question that people have been asking is why? This book offers a different answer to this question than other books have hypothesized.

This book is based on Dewayne's experiences and his own life. Readers get a glimpse at the early history of the Church of the Firstborn of the Fulness of Times, including how it formed and how and why it grew into one of the largest fundamentalist groups at the time. In fact, even today, the various offshoots of the CFBFT comprise one of the largest fundamentalist groups in Mormondom.

The book examines the relationship between Joel and Ervil and provides insight into why Ervil could turn so evil. Readers can feel the hurt that Ervil must have felt with the betrayal we read about here.

No legitimate study of Mormon Fundamentalism and its effects can ignore the contributions of Joel and Ervil LeBaron. Their relationship and their falling out left an indelible mark on Mormondom that still reverberates today. This book provides all of this and more. I think this story is worthy of your time and money. It will certainly get your mind thinking and that's always a good thing.

Fort Woods

Table of Contents

Foreword 6

Prologue – Setting the Stage 11

Chapter One - Required History 19

Chapter Two - The Mexican Connection 33

Chapter Three - Margarito Bautista 41

Chapter Four - Heber J. Grant Declares War 47

Chapter Five - Ervil & Joel, Joel & Ervil 53

Chapter Six - Ben LeBaron 57

Chapter Seven - The Fundamentalist Years 63

Chapter Eight - Economic Impacts 69

Chapter Nine - The LeBarons Start a Church or Two 75

Chapter Ten - Early Growth of the Church in Mexico and French Missionaries 89

Chapter Eleven - Rapid Growth and Problems 97

Chapter Twelve - About Me 107

Chapter Thirteen - Why I Left the LDS Church 117

Chapter Fourteen - I Joined The Church of the First Born of the Fulness of Times (CFBFT) 125

Chapter Fifteen - Plural Marriage 137

Chapter Sixteen - Bill Tucker 143

Chapter Seventeen - Reality Begins 149

Chapter Eighteen - Money, Women, Greed, and Other Problems 159

Chapter Nineteen - Captain Midnight: Money, Cars, Dope, and Guns 173

Chapter Twenty - Ervil Had the Aces, Joel had a Royal Flush, But the Game Was Over 177

Chapter Twenty-One - The 1974 Christmas Massacre 185

Epilogue – Going Forward 201

Notes and References 217

APPENDIX I - Ordination of Margarito Bautista 219

APPENDIX II - 60 Questions 221

APPENDIX III - On Ross and Joel 231

Prologue – Setting the Stage

Figure 1 *The Ervil LeBaron That I Knew*

Most of us have heard the name of Ervil LeBaron: the Mormon Manson, the Prophet of Blood, the Cain who murdered his brother. In the 1970's and 1980's, he was responsible for the death of an estimated thirty-three victims, slain in the United States and Mexico. Many were his own followers, immediate family, and relatives.

Why bring up this old story after so many years? First, because it has been reported incorrectly. Most authors have been guilty of an attribution bias. They have blamed personal or inborn genetic qualities and ignored the situational factors that formed Ervil's personality. This erroneous telling has negatively affected many people. With his thirteen wives, he fathered more than fifty children. Most of these children have been judged and traumatized simply because they are Ervil's descendants and the misattributed emphasis on genetically induced insanity. Because of whom their father was, they have led a difficult and negatively impacted life. Many of them were so young that they never knew him. Some don't carry the LeBaron name. Even when people do not know Ervil was their father, his children do, and it hurts. I share grandchildren and great-grandchildren with him, so I have personal knowledge of that trauma.

This is an attempt to understand how a loving, self-sacrificing, devoutly religious, individual changed and became a mass murderer. It is an attempt to understand Ervil LeBaron.

Others have written about what I am going to tell you. Most have engaged in speculation and sensationalization. What I am writing first is the verifiable history needed to understand the situational effect, then the pertinent facts to which I have personal knowledge of. I do not need to speculate or invent as so many have. The facts are sensational enough.

What are my qualifications for this?

I first met Ervil in 1963. I personally witnessed many of the things that I believe led to his insanity. Because of family ties I have knowledge of other influences. I was an active member of what was known as the Standing High Council for his brother Joel's church. That leadership position allowed me to see and hear for myself things that many have only been able to speculate about. Some of those things led me to join Ervil's dissident church in its infancy. This was before the killings began. I later had a personal epiphany that showed me where his church was going. It frightened me into leaving immediately. I publicly renounced him and again aligned myself with the church headed by his brother Joel LeBaron.

After Joel's, the brother of Ervil, murder, Ervil spent months evading capture. The knowledgeable, viable witnesses left the country to investigate some property in a remote area of Nicaragua. Knowing this, Ervil seized on a quirk in Mexican law. As soon as an accused person is in custody sufficient evidence for an indictment must be presented within a small, 72-hour window of time. Realizing the impossibility of anyone returning quickly, Ervil turned himself into the authorities. He thought no one was available to testify against him.

But I was.

I testified with enough evidence to indict him. He was held for trial until those with more evidence could return, resulting in his conviction. Overturning his conviction required a substantial bribe. These things put me among those he ordered killed as a required "blood atonement".

Ervil's followers attempted to "blood atone" me in 1974 during the "Los Molinos Christmas Massacre". Believing I was home, his followers firebombed my house, killed two people, and wounded thirteen others who attempted to save my house. That story has never been told accurately either.

Many people have told the Ervil LeBaron story in a way to make themselves look good and others look bad. Some facts have been obscured or inaccurately depicted. Some wrote their versions plagiarizing those untrue stories, usually with added speculation and dramatization. Some have written seeking sympathy, fame, and fortune. These are the worst because they are the furthest from the truth. Unfortunately, they are now considered historically accurate.

They are not even close to accurate, but history is established by those who write.

Since those stories of Ervil's history are so biased, I feel it is my obligation to write the story from an alternative position. I hope to show what made him become a psychopathic killer. And show how much of it was our fault; Yes, ours. We, the fanatic followers who parked our brains, sacrificed our integrity, aiding and abetting the transition into insanity by blindly following him and our other ecclesiastical leaders. We believed we were doing God's will.

I am an old man and have outlived most, if not all the people I will write about. They can neither confirm nor rebut anything I tell you. Group memories and reminiscences have demonized Ervil and deified his brother Joel. Many of the things I tell you will challenge the written and oral histories. Their followers and descendants may take offense at what I tell you. Some will say I have it wrong because their now-deceased relative told them differently or they read a book.

Long ago, I learned that just because it is in a book doesn't make it true. I also learned that memories are easily modified, usually without intention. People believe their modified memories, so they are not knowingly telling a lie.

All I can say about the things I tell you is that I was there. These will be my personal, first-hand impressions, understandings, and observations.

I have kept private notes over the years. It seems I have been preparing to write this for at least fifty years. I have made several attempts to explain, understand, and learn from what happened to Ervil. Fortunately, in this information age, I have been able to preserve those attempts. This has kept my memories from fading or changing, as memories often do for most people. The only modifications to my memories are details that I did not know or misunderstood at the time I wrote them down. If I somehow have something wrong, I welcome corrections.

The world has no shortage of religious and political fanatics. Mormonism has produced more than its share of leaders who have abused their position. They and their followers, believing themselves to be guided by God, have done unthinkable things. The history of religion is filled with horrors committed in the name of God. We need to examine and learn what factors lead to these atrocities.

Perhaps more importantly, we need to look at how these leaders attract and control their followers. And how their faithful followers encourage them to become more fanatical. There seems to be a synergetic relationship. If the leader is abusive, the followers either become surrogate abusers or willing victims. This, in turn, encourages the leaders to become more abusive.

Without willing followers, there can be no empowered leaders.

To my knowledge, Ervil never killed anyone himself. It was all done in the name of God by his fanatically obedient followers.

Hopefully, by reading this, we can gain some understanding. We can then avoid becoming those people who abandon their intelligence and integrity to follow the dictates of a self-proclaimed prophet of God. More importantly, we can cease to be enablers, justifying and supporting the actions of these abusive individuals.

> "All mass movements generate in their adherents a readiness to die and a proclivity for united action; all of them, irrespective of the doctrine they preach and the program they project,
> breed fanaticism, enthusiasm, fervent hope, hatred, and intolerance; all of them are capable of releasing a powerful flow of activity in certain departments of life; all of them demand blind faith and singlehearted allegiance. " (Hoffer, 1951)

Chapter One - Required History

We are all products of our environment. The environment that shaped Ervil was a particularly convoluted one. I will attempt to unravel it and show how it impacted him. I will look at religious, political, economic, and family influences and his interaction with the early 20th-century Mormon cultures in the United States and Mexico. I will also examine the influence of the Mormon fundamentalist mindset upon him.

I will start here.

In 1852, Orson Pratt presented to the world what became Doctrine and Covenants section 132. Plural marriage was out of the closet. The first six verses made it clear that the Mormon people must live it.

> 1 Verily, thus saith the Lord unto you my servant Joseph, that inasmuch as you have inquired of my hand to know and understand wherein I, the Lord, justified my servants Abraham, Isaac, and Jacob, as also Moses, David and Solomon, my servants, as touching the principle and doctrine of their having many wives and concubines

2 Behold, and lo, I am the Lord thy God, and will answer thee as touching this matter.

3 Therefore, prepare thy heart to receive and obey the instructions which I am about to give unto you; **for all those who have this law revealed unto them must obey the same.**

4 For behold, I reveal unto you a new and an everlasting covenant; and if ye abide not that covenant, then are ye damned; for no one can reject this covenant and be permitted to enter into my glory.

5 For all who will have a blessing at my hands shall abide the law which was appointed for that blessing, and the conditions thereof, as were instituted from before the foundation of the world.

6 And as pertaining to the new and everlasting covenant, it was instituted for the fulness of my glory; and **he that receiveth a fulness thereof must and shall abide the law, or he shall be**

damned, saith the Lord God. (DC 132: 1-6).

The non-Mormon world was shocked, appalled, and disgusted. They reacted negatively. Laws were passed. People were fined and imprisoned. Polygamous members lost the vote. The church had its property seized. In 1890 the church capitulated. It published a public document stating that the church would no longer sanction plural marriage. The 1890 Manifesto became the official church position on plural marriage. Church members were told to abandon the practice. (The most convenient source for this document is any LDS edition of the Doctrine and Covenants published since 1908 as Official Declaration and in the 1981 edition as Official Declaration-1.)

But sanctioned plural marriages continued.

Many church leaders while parroting the no more plural marriage rhetoric continued to live with their plural wives and entered into secret new plural marriages (Quinn, 1985). The Mormon Fundamentalist movement began during this era of conflicting realities and instructions. On the one hand, the church members wanted to follow the often vague and ambiguous advice of their leaders.

But they also wanted to follow the scriptures. Those scriptures were directly opposed to what their leaders were telling them.

Because of the Manifesto and the official instruction some polygamists abandoned their plural families. Most continued to support their wives and children but did not initiate new plural marriages. I am proud that none of my ancestors abandoned or shunned their plural wives and children. My great-grandfather, Warren Johnson, was typical. Upon learning of the manifesto, he spent several days and nights alone in the hills near his home. He prayed and debated with God and the devil. No rest or nourishment as he sought an answer. When he returned home, he is quoted as saying: "It is addressed to whom it may concern. Well, it does not concern me." (Johnson Family Files) He kept his wives. Many of his children became part of the post-manifesto polygamist communities.

Plural marriage never really ended. It just went underground.

Because one could be arrested for cohabitation, many hid their plural wives. Wives became "sisters", "aunts", and "unwed mothers". Fathers became "uncles". Children often used only their mother's last name. Some polygamists moved to Mexico or Canada.

In 1903 The United States Senate refused to seat Apostle Reed Smoot (Committee on Privileges and Elections, 1905). This was because plural marriage was rumored to have continued among the LDS leaders. More than a rumor, this was a fact. Church President Joseph F. Smith was subpoenaed to appear before the US Senate for questioning about this. While under oath he admitted it was true.[5] He then issued a second manifesto that again prohibited plural marriages. The church enforced it by excommunicating those who "got caught" performing, entering, or encouraging new plural marriages.

But plural marriage continued.

Even President Smith continued to live with his five plural wives. In 1906, he was brought to trial on a charge of unlawful cohabitation. He pleaded guilty and paid a fine.

He was a good role model for other polygamists.

In 1905 two members of the Quorum of the Twelve, John W. Taylor and Matthias F. Cowley, "got caught" and were forced to resign. John W. Taylor attempted to defend himself by presenting a copy of a revelation attributed to his father. The Quorum of Twelve Apostles rejected it and demanded his resignation. As near as I can tell from current investigations concerning the provenance of the revelation, it was genuine. It was in the handwriting of President John Taylor. It just was not politically appropriate at the time.

And I am not sure that even today the LDS church has accepted its authenticity.

John W. Taylor kept a copy of his father's revelation. It slowly went out to those who would keep celestial plural marriage alive.

The Revelation: Given to President John Taylor September 27, 1886

> "My son John, you have asked me concerning the New and Everlasting Covenant how far it is binding upon my people.
> Thus saith the Lord: All commandments that I give must be obeyed by those calling themselves by my name unless they are revoked by me or by my

authority, and how can I revoke an everlasting covenant, for I the Lord am everlasting and my everlasting covenants cannot be abrogated nor done away with, but they stand forever.

Have I not given my word in great plainness on this subject? Yet have not great numbers of my people been negligent in the observance of my law and the keeping of my commandments, and yet have I borne with them these many years; and this because of their weakness—because of the perilous times, and furthermore, **it is more pleasing to me that men should use their free agency in regard to these matters.** Nevertheless, I the Lord do not change and my word and my covenants and my law do not, and as I have heretofore said by my servant Joseph: **All those who would enter into my glory must and shall obey my law.** And have I not commanded men that if they were Abraham's seed and would enter into my glory, they must do the works of Abraham. **I have not**

revoked this law, nor will I, for it is everlasting, and those who will enter into my glory must obey the conditions thereof; even so, Amen" [8].

This 1886 revelation became the most important source of direction for the early fundamentalists. The phrase: "it is more pleasing to me that men should use their free agency in regard to these matters." solved the dilemma of scripture versus church authority. This document was so important that it was copied into the personal histories written by my polygamous ancestors and their associates. It was their justification for unanimously rejecting any politically motivated "manifesto".

In 1918 Joseph F. Smith died.

Heber J. Grant became President of the LDS Church. Grant has been described as a proud, arrogant individual. He is remembered for his determination to better himself through dedication to hard work, duty, honor, and service. He was a self-made man. He was ordained a Seventy at fifteen years of age and as an Apostle at twenty-five. He embodied the pioneer spirit. His firm voice, his perfect posture, and his forceful rhetoric demonstrated strength and determination. He is credited with many improvements to the LDS church.

He himself had once been arrested and required to pay a fine for having three plural wives. But by the time he became church president in 1918 only his second wife, Augusta Winters, was still living.

The no-nonsense Grant decided to put a stop to plural marriages. Not only did he cooperate with federal law enforcement, but he also demanded that local law enforcement arrest those who continued to marry plural wives.

Despite Grant's campaign, plural marriage was alive and well.

During a visit to Salt Lake City, Alma Dayer LeBaron received a copy of the 1886 Taylor revelation from ex-Apostle John W. Taylor. He had known Apostle Taylor from his years in Mexico and had questioned him about how he was able to live plural marriage even though it was forbidden. Convinced but still unsure about how to proceed, he asked his wife to legally divorce him while remaining his wife. It was sometime later and required a vision where his grandfather Benjamin F.

Johnson revealed to him the necessity to proceed. In December of 1923 he married Onie Jones as a plural wife. Dayer (as most people called him) and his wives Maude and Onie were promptly excommunicated in February of 1924. They were forced to flee to Mexico to avoid being arrested. He traveled in one direction. Maude and Onie in another. Told as a typical LeBaron narrative, there was an agent following them and several waiting at every corner ready to arrest them. They were not reunited until everyone was safely across the border (LeBaron, 1981).

In 1924 Dayer's brother, Grover Cleveland LeBaron, married my mother's oldest sister, Annie Spencer as a plural wife. Annie thoroughly believed in the principle of plural marriage. Because of Grant's anti-plural marriage campaign being a plural wife was not easy. Lots of hiding, separation, and denial of her marriage until they left Utah and moved to central Arizona.

A year or so later, my grandfather Isaac Carling Spencer moved to Chihuahua where he was initially a neighbor of Dayer LeBaron. Isaac and his wife Lydia Johnson Spencer operated a hotel in Dublan, a

Mormon colony near Casas Grandes. In 1928, Lydia chose and persuaded Sylvia Allred to become her husband's plural wife. Due to the 1929 economic depression, they soon left Mexico. They moved first to Lee's Ferry and then to Short Creek (now Colorado City), Arizona. Lydia moved on to Glendale, Utah, but was often in Short Creek. She helped with the children and served as the midwife for the birth of Sylvia's children. Unable to live together because of the fear of arrest, they still sustained each other. In 1983 I was fortunate to visit with Grandma Sylvia. She was living in Glendale and had only good things to say about Grandma Lydia. She also said that marrying my grandfather was the best decision she ever made.

During the 1920's polygamists began to coalesce around certain leaders. Many of them, even those with opposing claims, became associated with Nathanial Baldwin and his Baldwin Radio Company. In 1922 the following plural marriage advocates and practitioners were listed as company directors: former Apostle Matthias F. Cowley, John Y. Barlow, Israel Barlow, Ianthus Barlow, Albert Barlow, Lyman Jessop, Joseph S. Jessop, Moroni Jessop, Margarito Bautista, Leslie Broadbent, Joseph W. Musser, Lorin

C. Woolley John T. Clark, Clyde Neilson, Daniel Bateman, Paul Feil (Singer, 1979).

Lorin Woolley told of secret ordinations. In 1914, his father had been excommunicated for performing unauthorized plural marriages. Lorin claimed that prior to that, Joseph Smith and Jesus Christ had appeared in his father's home and commanded John Taylor to ordain men including Lorin and his father to continue plural marriage. His story prevailed. He ordained six men to become members of a council of seven High Priest Apostles with himself as the senior member. Between 1929 and 1933, he ordained Leslie Broadbent, John Y. Barlow, Joseph Musser, Charles F. Zitting, Legrand Woolley, and Louis Kelsch.

These seven men became known as the Council of Friends, each holding the newly minted office of High Priest Apostle, an office superior to that of the LDS First Presidency and the Council of Twelve.

Before this council could be announced to the world, they needed to formulate a priesthood platform. Musser and Broadbent did that with the publication of New and Everlasting Covenant of Marriage (1933) Supplement to a New and

Everlasting Covenant of Marriage (1934), and Priesthood Items (1934).

The Council of Friends became the governing ecclesiastical body for most Mormon fundamentalists. They were tasked with keeping plural marriage alive. They were told not to organize as a church but to remain with the church and support its leaders. But they did eventually organize a church, which then split into several competing ones. Each claiming to be headed by a "One Man" at a time and proclaiming that "mine house is a house of order...and not a house of confusion" (D&C 132:8). Each being the "One" and all the others being "out of order."

How confusing is that?

Chapter Two - The Mexican Connection

In Mexico, the 1913-1917 Mexican Revolution (Agrarian reform) brought about the Constitution of 1917. It disenfranchised all churches in Mexico. No anti-clerical enforcement action was taken until the 1924 election of the atheist Plutarco Elias Calles. Calles applied anti-clerical laws stringently throughout the country. In 1926 he added his own anti-clerical legislation: the "Law for Reforming the Penal Code", known unofficially as the "Calles Law". This provided specific penalties for priests and individuals who violated the provisions of the 1917 Constitution. All Mexican clerics were required to register, and all active foreign religious ministers were forced to leave Mexico (Schmal, 2019).

This would have been disastrous for the Mormon missionary efforts except for Mission President Rey Pratt. Through a delegation of authority, he was able to preside without appearing to preside. All conferences and meetings were presided over by local Mexican leaders. Pratt maintained contact, privately counseled and advised these leaders but never usurped their authority. He firmly believed in the value of delegated authority to cultivate leadership.

But on 14 April 1931, Rey Pratt died.

Antoine R. Ivins was appointed to succeed Pratt as president of the Mexican mission. Ivins spoke Spanish. He had spent many years as a teenager in the Mormon colonies. He had received much of his higher education in Mexico. He was an LDS general authority. He was the son of Anthony W. Ivins who had served for years in Mexico. He was a nephew of President Heber J. Grant.

He should have been perfect for the job. But he wasn't.

He ignored the members in Mexico. It would be almost a year before he even visited Mexico, and that would be under duress.

During this period, the local leaders were left to do the best they could. This was not a problem in the white-dominated northern Mormon colonies. It was viewed as a problem in the southern, primarily indigenous mission. Several conventions were held among the southern mission members. One of the things that they sought was for the LDS church to appoint Mexican leaders in accordance with Mexican law. Obeying the law should have made perfect sense because of Calles' extreme application of the 1917 Constitution.

But it didn't make sense to the white supremacist Ivins and Grant.

The Mexican Convention leaders sent letters to the church presidency asking for help. None were ever answered. They did prompt that initial visit from Ivins along with apostle Melvin J. Ballard. These two knew exactly how to handle the situation. They reprimanded convention leaders for their audacious behavior, reminded them of their racially inferior status as indigenous members, and hurried back to the US.

The Mexicans were left on their own. Surprisingly, they did well, adding many new members to the mission. This benign neglect lasted until 1934, when Ivins requested to be released. His replacement was Mexican-born Harold Wilcken Pratt.

At last, a Mexican-born mission President!

To bring the church into compliance with Mexican law, Pratt registered himself as a cleric. He then charged ahead enthusiastically. He worked tirelessly, efficiently, and very visibly. He presided over conferences. He reorganized branches. He purchased property for church building projects. He was doing a great job. But...

Many of the native Mexicans didn't like it.

After years of neglect, Pratt was too much, too fast. His dramatic assumption of leadership rapidly eliminated any hope for native (Lamanite) leadership. They had hoped for better opportunities to serve in leadership positions. Under their leadership, the mission had not failed but had prospered. Why did they need a white leader after they had proven their ability?

Pratt, noting how the mission had grown, proposed a division of the mission into both a Spanish-American (USA) and a Mexico mission. This brought about renewed hope and optimism among the Mexican members. Surely with a separate mission the church would appoint a real "Cara y Sangre" (brown face and indigenous blood) Lamanite to head the mission. This would bring about increased leadership opportunities for the Lamanite people.

But it didn't happen that way.

The mission did split, but the white Mexican citizen, Harold Pratt, remained as Mexican mission president. Not exactly what the brown Lamanites had hoped for.

Abel Paez, First Counselor in the Mexican District Presidency, called an extraordinary "crisis" conference. It became known as the "Third Convention". Many of the Mexican leaders were angry and rebellious. Even though they had been denied twice before, they decided to petition for a Lamanite mission president again. Abel Paez and more than 800 members didn't ask but demanded that their petitions be heard and a Lamanite mission president be appointed.

They felt that the Lamanite people were prophesied to take a leading role. They were very aware that the Book of Mormon promised this. They felt that for those prophecies to happen, they needed to escape the paternalistic, second-class, racist treatment that they had so far experienced from the authorities in Salt Lake City. These sentiments are probably best expressed in one of the papers that came out of the third convention:

"That the white race is our tutor we do not deny, but it is also true that at some point in time our tutor, by a humanitarian act, must set us free to develop our own selves ....The success or fruits of sixty years of our church's labor among us cannot be recognized until the moment that the church has sufficient faith to confer upon us the responsibility of guiding our own destinies for the development of our spiritual life and the redemption of our people..." (Informe general de la tercera convention, p. 20; (Tullis, 2018)).

All of this fell on the very deaf ears of LDS President Heber J. Grant. He may not have even understood it. He spoke no Spanish. He had no conception of Mexican values or aspirations. He was racist. He had no interest in sharing leadership with the lowly Mexicans. He knew that the Third Convention was out of order. Those who participated in it were just rebellious troublemakers. They deserved a severe rebuke. If the Third Convention was demanding that their petitions be heard, he knew exactly how to handle those demands. Just excommunicate the leaders. Let them know who was in charge.

The main leaders were excommunicated.

What Grant wasn't expecting was how loyal the members were to those leaders. Over a third of the southern Mexican mission followed them and separated from the church to begin their own version of Mormonism in Mexico. They would not return until after the death of Grant (Tullis & Hernandez, Mormons in Mexico: Leadership, Nationaism, and the Case of the Third Convention, 1987).

Chapter Three - Margarito Bautista

Figure 2 Margarito Bautista

Among those attending the Third Convention was Margarito Bautista, an uncle to Abel Paez. Bautista was the author of a popular and influential Spanish language book that told of the glorious future prophesied for the Lamanite people. He is of particular interest because of his future influence on Ervil. Also, without him, it is doubtful that there would be much, or any, present-day plural marriages among the Lamanites in Mexico.

Bautista converted to Mormonism at an early age. He traveled to Chihuahua and became acquainted with the local LDS people. He learned English from them. He then traveled to Arizona and Utah where he engaged in temple work. Once he settled in Salt Lake, he was a prime mover pushing for the establishment of a Spanish language group. Because of his activities, the church did establish a Spanish language branch. He became the first president of that branch.

During this time, he became acquainted with various fundamentalists and their sympathizers. Among these were men such as Nathanial Baldwin and Alma Dayer LeBaron Sr. Bautista showed no inclination to practice polygamy, but he certainly knew that it was continuing to be practiced, both in the US and Mexico.

In 1922, Bautista received a mission call to Mexico. Upon arriving in Mexico, he enthusiastically embraced the idea that Mexicans, not white foreigners, should oversee Mexican affairs. A well-read student of the scriptures, Bautista was very familiar with and believed the prophecies of the Book of Mormon. They predicted a time when the Lamanite people would receive the gospel in its fullness, including plural marriage. Not only would they receive it, but they would also take leadership roles. (3rd Nephi 16: 10-16). Rey Pratt and other Mormon leaders had often touched upon the theme of the Lamanites taking the leadership in the last days. 3rd Nephi predicts them displacing the white race.

If you read 3rd Nephi, be aware that the believing Gentiles are the Mormon people, and the Lamanites are the House of Israel in that book. Even Joseph Smith is referred to as a Gentile. (See the revelation used as the flyleaf of the BOM)

Bautista decided to write a book that drew heavily on those prophecies of 3rd Nephi. He related them to Old Testament themes. He had been encouraged by Rey Pratt, who wanted to see more gospel literature become available in Spanish. But Rey Pratt died before the book was finished. The book: La evolución de México: sus verdaderos progenitores y su origen; el destino de América y Europa. (In English: The Evolution in Mexico: its true protagonists and their origin, the fate of America and Europe).

Bautista returned to the US expecting church approval and financing for its publication. Most of the General Authorities did not speak or read Spanish. It was given to the newly appointed Mission President, Harold Pratt to read. He decided that the church should not publish it (Pratt, 1995).

Having read it, I would have agreed with Pratt. But the Lamanites loved it.

In 1934, after denial for church publication, Bautista returned to Mexico and published 7,000 copies himself (Pulido, 2020). The book rapidly gained wide circulation among Mexican Mormons. They read the book with an emotional pride engendered by its rendering of their ancestral history and its proclamations of great future events to be brought about by their people. Since it portrayed them as the future saviors of the gospel and Latin America, it gave them great hope for a better life.

Alarmed that the book was confusing Bautista's doctrines with those of the church, Pratt issued a letter stating that the church had not authorized the book. Its contents were in no way church doctrine. The missionaries were told to counsel members "not to buy the book and not to read it."

Relations between Pratt and Bautista quickly deteriorated.

After the separation from the church by the members affiliated with the Third Convention, Margarito Bautista proposed living the fullness of the Gospel. That included plural marriage and united order. Many in the Third Convention were unwilling to embrace either of those doctrines. Bautista separated from that group also. He was determined to live the fullness of the Gospel.

The LDS church under President George Albert Smith eventually reconciled with the members of the third convention but not with Bautista. He went on to establish a group near Ozumba, Mexico. This was on less than eight acres of land he purchased from one of his sisters. Bautista laid out a community he named Colonia Industrial. He later acquired additional land for farming. Everyone was put under a strict covenant to live the United Order. He soon instituted a form of plural marriage with him deciding who could and couldn't practice it.

(Incidentally, Bautista had another sister, Margarita, who was the grandmother of my wife Oralia. For some time, we thought Margarito and Margarita must be twins. But no. She was older. They just had the same saint day. Naming in Catholic Mexico can be easy. Just check which Saint owns the birth date.)

Bautista had been in contact with the fundamentalist movement from the beginning. Joseph Musser and Rulon Allred became aware of his success with the Lamanite people. In 1951, they visited Ozumba. Musser and Allred ordained him as a High Priest Apostle and a member of their priesthood council. He was put in charge of the Latin American people, including the LeBarons. Part of his commission reads:

> "You are over the Latin American people to continue the fullness of the gospel and the ordinances among them, without having to depend on any other man," (See full ordination in Appendix)

As others have surmised, Margarito appreciated the recognition and ordination but didn't think it was needed. He was a native-born Lamanite. He considered the priesthood he already held and his birthright as a Lamanite to be sufficient. He believed priesthood should be patrilinear as in the Old Testament. The ordination and the recognition by the fundamentalist leaders were just icing on the cake.

Chapter Four - Heber J. Grant Declares War

By the 1930's Grant was officially at war with the polygamists. He encouraged church members to spy and report on their neighbors. He even instituted a loyalty oath for suspected polygamists.

> "We have been, and we are willing to give such legal assistance as we legally can in the criminal prosecution of such cases. We are willing to go to such limits not only because we regard it as our duty as citizens of the country to assist in the enforcement of the law and the suppression of pretended "plural marriages" but also because we wish to do everything humanly possible to make our attitude toward this matter clear, definite, and unequivocal as to leave no possible doubt of it in the mind of any person" (Official Statement on Plural Marriage, April 4, 1931," in Conference Reports)

The church-compliant Utah Legislature soon passed a new law. It made unlawful cohabitation a felony, effective May 15, 1935.

However, it was the State of Arizona that the church used to punish certain members in 1935. First, Grant imposed his loyalty oath. After most of the members at Short Creek, Arizona refused to sign Grant's loyalty oath, they were excommunicated and their ward was dissolved.

Claud Hirschi, President of Zion Park Stake then sent their names to the Mohave County Prosecutor at Kingman. He requested that the civil authorities do their duty and send them to prison. Since most of the submitted names were not living plural marriage, the first attempt at prosecution failed.

Later, Mohave County Prosecutor Bollinger signed warrants for the arrest of six known polygamists living in the community. They were my maternal grandfather Isaac Carling Spencer, Sylvia Allred Spencer, Price W. Johnson, Helen Hull Johnson, John Y. Barlow, and Mary Roe Barlow. Of these, only Isaac Carling Spencer, his wife Sylvia Allred Spencer, and Isaac's brother-in-law Price Johnson met the requirements for a formal accusation and trial. Possibly because they proudly admitted to breaking the law to live according to their religious beliefs.

Nothing quite like becoming willing martyrs for their beliefs.

But instead of sainthood, they each received a two-year sentence in the Arizona State prison at Florence. AZ. Sylvia's was suspended because she was due to deliver a child. Even the judge wasn't willing to see her imprisoned just because she married my grandfather.

Under Heber J. Grant the church changed from persecuted to persecutor.

Grant had imposed his loyalty oath leading to mass excommunications without a hearing. This included non-polygamists. Who needs a trial anyway? They were obviously guilty by association and insubordination since they refused to sign the loyalty oath.

Grant succeeded in getting some polygamists arrested and imprisoned. He dissolved several wards because he believed they were infiltrated with believers in plural marriage.

As previously discussed, he alienated and lost a large portion of the Mexican mission, not because of even a hint of plural marriage but because of rebellion and insubordination. I suppose that in his mind those ignorant brown peasants were trying to tell him how to run the church in Mexico.

What they were trying to do was to get the church to obey the Mexican laws by allowing a Lamanite to lead them.

One of the stated objectives of the early fundamentalist movement was not to organize. They had intended to remain loyal to the church and participate as best they could. Heber J. Grant's campaign changed that in two ways. He was determined to drive them out of the church and one of the results of his efforts was the hardening of the resolve to live plural marriage. This led to the formal organization of the fundamentalists in the US and the birth of a fundamentalist group in Mexico.

Historians Martha S, Bradley, and Cristina Rosetti have posited that it was Grant's opposition that brought about the unyielding rejection of his efforts.

> "Those ostracized from their mother church grouped together to form a new order." The loyalty oaths and subsequent excommunications were reciprocal modes of identity formation. Excommunication placed the

polygamous Mormons outside of the church, while simultaneously forging an outsider identity that slowly became a point of celebration." (Martha S. Bradley)

"...these same efforts forged a new Mormonism that became increasingly entrenched throughout the twentieth century. Through excommunication and enacted loyalty to their priesthood over their institution, polygamous Mormons constructed themselves not merely as outsiders, but as the faithful." (Cristina Rosetti)

Besides, the fundamentalists were convinced that Grant, and those who followed as presidents of the church, were surely "in league" with the devil.

"But suppose that this Church should give up this holy order of marriage, then would the devil, and all who are in league with him against the cause of God, rejoice that they had prevailed upon the Saints to refuse to obey one of the revelations and commandments of God to them." (Brigham Young June 1866)

Chapter Five - Ervil & Joel, Joel & Ervil

Now, we need to learn some things about Joel and Ervil LeBaron.

Joel Franklin LeBaron was born July 9, 1923, in LaVerkin, Utah, and Ervil Morrell LeBaron was born February 22, 1925, in Colonia Juarez, Chihuahua, Mexico. The important fact here is that Ervil was a natural-born Mexican. Joel was an American. This gave Ervil special rights in Mexico that his older brother Joel didn't have. One right in particular is important to know so you can understand significant events that played a part in Ervil's transformation.

Property ownership in Mexico has a long and abused history with the Catholic Church and foreign investors sometimes owning most of the land. That was what the 1915-1917 revolution (Agrarian Reform) was about. It brought about the Constitution of 1917. Consequently, no church can own any real property in Mexico. No foreigner can own any land within 50 kilometers (about 31 miles) from shorelines and 100 kilometers (about 62 miles) from international borders.

Since the church could not own any land, all "church" property that the Church of the First Born of the Fulness of Times (CFBFT) owned was legally the property of individuals, usually a LeBaron. Joel, as an American, could and did own extensive personal and "church" land in Chihuahua. In Baja California, the "church" property was almost all owned by Ervil, the Mexican.

Being close in age and with the younger Ervil being large for his age, Joel and Ervil were best friends. They were inseparable as children. So much so that friends and family looked upon them as a unit. Joel and Ervil, Ervil and Joel. You couldn't have one without the other. Ervil loved his brother Joel without any reservations, and he believed that Joel loved him unconditionally as well.

Even though their parents were out of the church, they were raised as Mormons. When Joel came of age, he received a mission call. Ervil was underage but couldn't bear the thought of not going with Joel. Special permission was sought and obtained. This by a personal interview with the then Apostle George Albert Smith. Ervil joined Joel on his mission in the south of Mexico. Two tall, blonde, white, Spanish-fluent young men. They were apparently good missionaries. Their family received good reports from both the LDS Mission President and Margarito Bautista, the leader of the fundamentalist group in Ozumba and a friend of their father.

But that changed.

Their older brother, Alma Dayer LeBaron Jr. had served in that same mission. He began to preach strong doctrines that offended the LDS church leadership. He was summoned to a disciplinary council. He sent a message to Joel and Ervil to hurry home and help him. They abandoned their mission without notice or permission and hurried home. All three were excommunicated.

The United States was involved in World War Two. No longer exempt as missionaries, the older American citizens were drafted. The Mexican citizen Ervil registered in Mexico City but apparently was never called. The American citizens Alma Dayer Jr. and Joel claimed conscientious objector status, relying upon DC 98:33

> "And again, this is the law that I gave unto mine ancients, that they should not go out unto battle against any nation, kindred, tongue, or people, save I, the Lord, commanded them".

56

They did go to jail for a while, but neither went to war. (The war was nearly over.)

Chapter Six - Ben LeBaron

We need to discuss the older brother Ben Teasdale LeBaron. Ben was the oldest of the brothers. He was smart. athletic, and popular enough to be elected student body president of the LDS Col. Juarez Academy. All the younger brothers looked up to him and followed his lead. He was fun and inventive of things to do. As the oldest brother, he was also good at mediating disputes and encouraging his younger brothers to excel.

Ben's father and mother held high expectations for their children. His mother was particularly demanding of excellence from her children. Everyone was expected to play an instrument. Her daughters won contests at piano recitals. Ben was extremely proud of his grades and success in the Glee Club in college. He had worked his way through college as a successful Fuller Brush salesman and even owned his own car. He was the pride and joy of his father and mother.

But as he approached graduation from college, some things went wrong in his life. He soon experienced some severe disappointments.

First, his mother sent a letter where she complained to him about how mistreated she was by his father. He hurried home, took her side, and severely criticized his father, only to discover that he had overreacted. His mother and dad were doing just great and were very affectionate with each other.

Ben felt he had been made into a fool.

But he would still soon graduate from Gila Jr. College. He fully expected to marry and have a great life. But his fiancé abandoned him and married someone else. His esteem suffered a massive hit. As strong and intelligent as he was, he couldn't deal with his being made foolish by his parents and the rejection by his fiancé. This inability to deal with rejection and disappointment is important to note. With the high expectations of success instilled and demanded by his parents and the unexpected failure of those hopes and expectations, something snapped.

He went into a state of depression. He suffered what they called a nervous breakdown. He began to suffer from delusions. He soon declared himself to be the "One Mighty and Strong" of the LDS Doctrine and Covenants Section 85. Ben set out to find some converts. He was still rational enough to convince several. He did manage to marry and father some children.

While Joel was in the US dealing with his draft problems, Ben moved his family to Mexico. Soon, Ervil and Alma Jr. accepted his claims and became devoted followers. They were joined in Mexico by a few converts, including their cousin Owen LeBaron and Joseph Marston. They all believed Ben was indeed that anticipated prophet who would set the house of God in order. Ervil sincerely believed that Ben was a prophet. He plunged fully into a campaign of preaching and printing. He translated fundamentalist Mormon writings into Spanish. Things written by Ben and Owen drew heavily on fundamentalist publications such as Truth Magazine and made sense to many people. On his own press (supplied by Joseph Marston) Ervil printed the things they wrote and that he felt would enlighten the public.

Ben was noted for being very demanding. His clothing had to be perfect. His food had to be prepared exactly the way he wanted it. He demanded total obedience from his followers. Ervil would later demand the same.

Some of Ben's demands were bizarre. For example, Alma was his right apostle, and Ervil was his left apostle. Alma always sat on his right, and Ervil always sat on his left. Ben's number one apostle was his cousin Owen. He could sit at Ben's feet or even on his lap. Joe Marston provided financial support. Marston's job was to "milk the gentiles" (Bronson, et al., 1958). I don't know where he was allowed to sit. Maybe on a milk stool.

I don't know that, but it is the kind of thing Ben might demand.

One of Ben's most reported actions was when he decided to prove that he was the one mighty and strong. He journeyed to Salt Lake City. He held up traffic while he did pushups in the middle of a busy intersection on State Street. He is reported to have challenged the policeman who came to take him away to do the same. He did end up in the local insane asylum. Soon he and his cousin Owen were both confined. After years of sacrifice and seeing both Ben and Owen committed to the insane asylum, Ervil finally realized that Ben and Owen were not God's servants.

Years later, I met Ben. He was designing and building the windmills that gave Los Molinos its

Figure 3 The Windmills at Los Molinos

name, and I was helping him and visiting with him. He asked me: "DeWayne, do you know what is the best thing about being crazy? You can say anything you want to. You can even tell the truth."

He didn't seem that crazy to me.

Ervil learned some very negative things from Ben and Owen. They were abusive men. They treated everyone as inferior, especially the women. They also demanded strict obedience.

Additionally, Ervil's father Alma Dayer Sr. was a harsh disciplinarian. My mother was their neighbor in Mexico when she was 8 years old. She remembered him as "The meanest son of a bitch I ever met". She was traumatized by the way he treated his children, especially her friend Lucinda, who had some mental and emotional challenges.

Chapter Seven - The Fundamentalist Years

Although Ervil had passed through a severe and traumatic experience with Ben and Owen, he did not lose his desire to serve the Lord's cause. He soon joined the fundamentalists led by Musser and Bautista. He devoted all his time and energy to serving them. He was one hundred percent committed and spent his time preaching, translating, and publishing fundamentalist documents into Spanish.

Ervil donated his time and any money he could get to forward the work of whatever church he was affiliated with. He had worked tirelessly for his brother Ben, translating and printing literature at great personal sacrifice. He did the same when he supported the efforts of Joseph Musser and Margarito Bautista. Like a medieval monk, Ervil has been described as sitting wrapped in a blanket working in inadequate light while he painstakingly penned a pamphlet or translation (LeBaron, 1981).

One of the many documents he was translating deserves special mention. It was a pamphlet authored by Joseph White Musser and J. Leslie Broadbent. It was called "A Priesthood Issue". His father Dayer forbade him to finish the translation stating:

> "Now I can see why I was so strongly impressed to come over here this morning. That pamphlet is not supposed to go out to the Lamanite people because there are some very serious fallacies in it. If you do publish it, someone will have to come later with more knowledge and overthrow the doctrine it contains." (LeBaron, 1981)

This incident is important because the document influenced Ervil's later document "Priesthood Expounded" written for the Church of the Firstborn of the Fulness of Times. Today, Priesthood Expounded is considered a canonized scripture within Joel's church. It is full of errors, but most members of the CFBFT think Joel wrote it. They have even hidden Ervil's name on it.

From Bautista, Ervil may have learned techniques he later used to attract and marry young women.

Bautista's first plural wife was thirty-seven years younger than him. He courted her in opposition to her father's prohibition and insistence that they maintain a platonic relationship. He agreed but continued to court her romantically. After being caught, she broke up with him. But he continued to pursue her and was successful. She would break up with him many times, but he would convince her to continue. He would shame her and insist that the problem was her fault due to her inability to humble herself, commit to him, and convince her parents (Pulido, 2020).

Bautista liked younger women. (Don't we all? But not that young.) He married very young women. He controlled them through indoctrination and shaming them for even minor offenses.

Just to avoid the pedophile label, we need to understand that marriages to pre-pubescent girls were normal and accepted among the indigenous people in Bautista's area. They usually continued to live with their parents until they matured, then they would move in with their husbands. Their marriages were not consummated until after puberty. Since he was the leader, these marriages were an honor for the girl and her family.

After establishing his group in Ozumba, Bautista controlled all plural marriages within that group, and he instituted restrictions for the men. They must first find, convert, and marry someone from outside of the group. Only then could they qualify to court the young women within the group. Those young women were reserved for the older, married, and worthy men. He, of course, was the worthiest, so he had the first pick. None of this was lost on Ervil.

Joseph Musser was totally against that type of controlled marriage. But he was the author of a horrible doctrine called the Law of Purity. According to the Law of Purity, the only excuse for sex is for children. It was practiced among the fundamentalists, including Ervil's father and brothers.

Here you thought plural marriage was all about sex. Maybe it is, but not in the way you thought. Among the fundamentalists, the "Law of Purity" can easily become a control mechanism.

Among monogamists, the women often use sex to control the men. Among polygamists, the men often use it to control the women.

Ervil used this as a control mechanism. Ervil once told me: "Never give a wife as much sex as she wants because you will lose control of her." As odd as that seems, the idea is to keep her off balance. She will try to do better to please her husband. Ervil learned many abusive mind-control techniques from these men.

The Fundamentalist Church split with my grandmother's little brother LeRoy Johnson taking control of the Short Creek Group (FLDS) and Joseph Musser controlling the rest. Musser appointed Rulon Allred to preside over the American group (AUB) and Margarito Bautista to preside over the Mexican group. The LeBaron, Spencer, and other fundamentalist families residing in Chihuahua fell under Bautista in terms of jurisdiction but with strong ties to the AUB and with both groups under Musser.

Ervil was part of that group, still devoted to translating and publishing documents for the Allred and Bautista segments. He even donated his beloved printing press to Bautista in Ozumba, Mexico.

Bautista later used it to print anti-LeBaron literature.

After Joel served his jail term, he returned to Mexico. He worked with his father. He also worked buying corn and other food items in the mountains of Chihuahua for resale. He rejoined the LDS church. He had managed to remain apart from most of his brother's religious activities. He apparently managed to avoid his Brother Ben's influence and domination completely.

Alma Dayer LeBaron Sr. died in February of 1951.

Later, because of a government freeze on the resale of corn, Joel's resale business failed. He joined his brothers in their United Order effort under Allred and Bautista. It was probably an economically motivated decision rather than a religious one.

Chapter Eight - Economic Impacts

Perhaps this is a good place to examine the economy during the time that Ervil and Joel grew up. It was during the great depression. No jobs. No money in circulation.

What do you do to stay alive and thrive in that situation?

If you had land, you could eat. If not, then you need to have some imagination and try different ways to make money. My mother married in 1935. Ross Wesley LeBaron had courted her. One of the big factors that helped her to choose my father was the economic depression. My father's family had farmland. They grew more food than they could eat. Fortunately, there were active mines within a few hundred miles. My father carried produce and other things to the mines and sold them for cash. Something that was very rare at the time. He was able to own his small truck and a car.

Ross, on the other hand, was trying to sell clothes door to door. In rural Utah at the time that wasn't all bad. Most people would buy from the Sears catalog when and if they had money. Having it at your door was a better choice. If you had any money, or if you could barter with the salesman, you might buy what was offered.

My mother: "I really liked Ross, but all he had was a suitcase full of neckties. Your dad had a truck and a roadster. I chose your dad." Tough times require tough decisions.

In Mexico, it was harder to get by. As late as the 1960's I was able to visit some of the indigenous people in Mexico. I remember visiting someone's relative in Chihuahua. They called her "Tia Frijolita" (Aunt Beans). She and her family ate beans three times a day. They were typical and not different from their neighbors. They had a small piece of land. They would plant corn, beans, and squash. When and if it rained, they would sprout and grow. These people had lived this way for centuries. Homemade tortillas, beans, and sometimes eggs, sometimes a small piece of chicken or rabbit, sometimes cactus (Nopal). Hardly ever beef. If they owned any cows, the calves were raised to maturity and sold to get enough cash to buy necessities such as coffee. Coffee cooked in a pot of water and then served black. Strain it with your teeth. Horrible stuff. Especially for a non-coffee drinking Mormon like me. I felt obligated to take what they gave me. It took me years for me to learn to appreciate coffee.

Irene Spencer, in her book Cult Insanity, claims Ervil was so poor that he used a piece of barbed wire to hold up his trousers. Typical of her books, I doubt it. Growing up or even as an adult, I've sometimes improvised a belt from a thin rope, even a piece of wire. And not because of poverty. Sometimes a belt or a buckle will just fail or get forgotten. (I didn't think these pants needed a belt, but the fabric stretched with use). But barbed wire? You must be kidding.

As a middle child, I'm sure he wore a lot of hand-me-downs. Even as the oldest in my family, I got them from cousins and uncles. Perhaps that is why he was so particular about his clothing later in life, or maybe he listened to his mother's advice on the value of appearance. Ben had that same desire for a perfect appearance for most of his adult life.

"If you are going to succeed in life, you must look successful."

Alma Dayer LeBaron Sr. was savvy enough to see an opportunity and grab it. He also had a small amount of capital and the ability to drive a bargain.

As cars began to replace wagons in the US he would buy, and transport used wagons to Mexico where they were still very much in style. When he wanted to plant orchards, he became a sales agent for fruit tree nurseries and sold trees to his neighbors. He took his commission in trees. He is credited with helping to establish the fruit and nut business so important to the economy of present-day Chihuahua.

His sons attempted various projects. Ben was a successful Fuller Brush salesman while in college. The younger sons weren't that fortunate. Many of their projects failed. Often from ignorance of what was required. A dairy and cheese-making project failed because their expensive, high-production cows didn't produce on a diet of native grass and weeds. They ended up returning those cows to their original owner in a terribly starved condition. Instead of a profit, they gained a debt with a big bill to pay.

Even when they succeeded, they were usually immediately copied by others until there was too much competition for resources. An example: Although the LeBarons were unable to succeed in the dairy business, others in their area were successful. Male calves are a drag on the dairy business, so they were of little value. The LeBarons were very successful with their goats. They started to buy the very cheap male calves and raise them on goat milk then sell them as beef. They were successful at this. The only problem was that many people saw that success and tried to do the same. Male calves skyrocketed in price. Soon, no one was making any money at this.

And failure due to unexpected government interference such as the government-imposed freeze on corn that put Joel out of business. Those were tough times. Joining in a United Order seemed to be a good idea, but lack of capital was still a problem.

In 1955, Joel, Verlan, and Floren caught a ride to Salt Lake City with one of the Allreds. Their specific purpose was to seek financial help from the Allred group for their United Order in Mexico. Like most of us in those times, they stayed with relatives rather than rent a room. The brothers stayed with their older brother Ross.

Their appeal for financial help failed. Verlan soon returned to Mexico.

Chapter Nine - The LeBarons Start a Church or Two

Joel and Floren ended up helping Ross LeBaron organize the Church of the Firstborn of the Fulness of Times (CFBFT)

Figure 4 The LeBaron Men

In his book "The LeBaron Story," Verlan repeatedly states that Joel didn't plan on going with them and "nothing Joel said or did indicated that he had gone to Utah for a special purpose." He steers completely away from the idea of financial help from the Allred group. After many pages of denial rhetoric, he has Joel saying: "Verlan, I never took one step toward

Utah until the Lord told me that the time had come to commence organizing the people and to do the work that was put upon me."

Verlan's efforts as an apologist for Joel would be great, except Floren kept notes during the organization of the CFBFT. Also, even a casual perusal of the Articles of Incorporation and Bylaws contradicts his story. In fact, in later years, the notes and legal papers would become an embarrassment to that narrative.

Ross wanted to organize a church along patriarchal (Family government) lines. The Church of the Firstborn of the Fulness of Time was organized on Sept 21, 1955. Ross heading the church as Patriarch in accordance with DC 124:124. Joel is in the subordinate office of President of the church.

Initially, it consisted of the three brothers. Ross Wesley, Joel, and Floren LeBaron. Just to make sure that everything was in order, Ross ordained Joel and Floren with all the keys and priesthood that he had received from his father. Joel then ordained Ross and Floren with all the keys and priesthood that he had received from his father. (Notes made by Floren LeBaron. 1955. Originals in my possession)

Most fundamentalists during that time were looking for the "One Mighty and Strong" or the "Indian Prophet" to appear. Joel promised to follow Ross's lead until such time as the "One Mighty and Strong" came on the scene.

That did not last long.

Joel and Ross had different agendas. They couldn't even agree on who was the Firstborn. Ross wanted to organize the Church of the Father or in other words, the Church of Exaltation. (The father being Adam, the firstborn of this earth) Joel wanted to re-organize the Church of Jesus Christ (the firstborn son of God) or the Church of Salvation along lines given by Joseph Smith with some crossover into the Church of the Father. There was conflict almost immediately.

Let's look at some forgotten, deleted, or obscured Mormon History.

Joseph Smith created a society that was unique and challenging to many Christian traditions and beliefs of his time. He organized three independent organizations to teach and govern this society.

First, he started a church of Jesus Christ dedicated to the restoration of principles that originated with

Jesus Christ. It was a church emphasizing the principles of faith, repentance, baptism, and the reception of the gift of the Holy Ghost. Its stated purpose was to bring about the salvation of all who subscribed to its tenets as a gift from Jesus Christ. The most important being Love of God and Love of Neighbor. The Holy Ghost was the source of revelation, inspiration, and instruction to every member. Members obtained the right to salvation through demonstrating that they were willing to live harmoniously in a society governed by the priesthood of God.

In summary: The primary purpose of the Church of Jesus Christ was to offer salvation to all mankind by teaching them the necessary social laws of love and respect which when incorporated into their lives enabled them to live in a state of harmony in the Kingdom of God. Through the atonement of Jesus Christ salvation was offered as a free gift to all who demonstrated their willingness to live according to those laws of love and respect

This was a revolutionary idea in 1830 when most Christians felt that God was beyond their reach. Revelation was dead.

The Church of Jesus Christ developed into a hierarchical organization featuring a division of authority and power outlined in DC 124: 123-145 where duties and responsibilities are specified. Each Officer's tenancy was dependent upon the common consent of its members. In 1836, Joseph Smith pronounced the organization of the church to be correct and complete.

On April 3rd, 1836, Joseph Smith and Oliver Cowdrey received a vision recorded as Section 110 in the Doctrine and Covenants. This vision resulted in Joseph Smith founding two additional organizations. Both were independent of the church of Christ and unknown to the majority of its members.

On March 17th, 1842, he participated in the organization of the Female Relief Society. This was, in many ways a precursor of the admittance of women into the Priesthood organization of the Church of Exaltation.

At a subsequent March 30th, 1842 meeting, Joseph Smith said: "The Society should move according to the ancient Priesthood, hence there should be a select Society separate from all the evils of the world, choice, virtuous and holy- Said he was going to make of this Society a kingdom of priests as in Enoch's day- as in Paul's day - that it is the privilege of each member to live long and enjoy health."

In a meeting on April 28th, 1842. President Smith arose and said that the purpose of his being present on the occasion was, to make observations respecting the Priesthood and give instructions for the benefit of the Society, that the keys of the kingdom are about to be given to them, that they may be able to detect everything false- as well as to the Elders. (The Joseph Smith Papers)

On May 4th, 1842, Joseph began the organization of the Church of Exaltation by conducting an endowment session in the upper part of the red brick store. He endowed 9 men as recorded on p. 237 of the TPJS or DHC 5:1-2. (Two men, William Marks and William Law, were removed from the record at Brigham Young's direction)

On Sept 28th, 1843, Joseph Smith and Emma became the first couple to receive their second anointings. Additional men and women received these ordinances resulting in about 20 recorded ordinations during Joseph's time. (Personal records indicate that there may have been more)

These couples were to be the core of the church of exaltation. It was a Patriarchal, Matriarchal organization. Each couple was to teach their children and at some point, administer the ordinances to their children. People who had no completely endowed parents were to be adopted as though they were equal to their other children. The adoptive parents were to teach them and take them through the temple ordinances, including the second anointing. This was not a separation from biological parents but more like the God Parent-God Child relationship in the Catholic church.

This resulted in a church with fully endowed people having the fullness of the priesthood linked back to Adam. Their priesthood being after the Order of God the Father, not after the Order of Jesus Christ. They were anointed as Kings and Priests, Queens and Priestesses in Israel, and ordained Patriarchs and Matriarchs after the Order of God the Father and Mother. They received the keys to revelation and the promise that whatever they bless on earth will be blessed in heaven as well as other blessings. (See Matthew 16: 16-19).

Joseph Smith was sustained as the head of the Church of Exaltation by common consent. The Church of Jesus Christ organization had nothing to do with this new organization.

The third independent organization was the one commonly referred to as the Council of Fifty. It was organized to guarantee and protect the rights of all people to freedom of religion. It included honorable men who were not associated with the church. It was not an ecclesiastical organization. It was a civil one.

The LDS church, from Brigham Young's administration until today, has followed a downward trajectory. Joseph Smith introduced ideas that were revolutionary for Christianity. He emphasized that early Christianity had apostatized from the teachings of Jesus Christ. His efforts are best described as a restoration. Some of his restorations didn't sit well with established Christianity. Joseph Smith's Church of Jesus Christ featured a balanced hierarchy with administrative power distributed between various quorums. When Joseph and Hyrum were assassinated, Brigham Young eliminated that balance of authority. He amalgamated the responsibilities and reasons for Joseph's three organizations. He established the idea that the Quorum of the Twelve Apostles held all power, with their senior apostle holding the keys to all blessings. The one man at a time theory was born. With time, the LDS church fell into apostasy. Today it is rapidly becoming a mainline Christian organization and losing its unique perspectives.

Ross was trying to reorganize the Church of Exaltation. Joel was trying to organize the Church of Salvation and later the civil organization. No one got it quite right, but the idea was there. I don't know of any other group in Mormonism that even begins to understand the concept. Ross did the best job of explaining it. But Ross has been judged as another crazy LeBaron.

Joel, not understanding what Ross was doing, declared that he was going into the mountains to fast and pray until he got some answers. Joel was given a ride up into Farmington Canyon, where he very quickly received a vision wherein heavenly messengers came and delivered keys and instructions to him. When he came down, he knew what he had to do. He also knew he was the "One

Mighty and Strong." This released him from his agreement with Ross.

Skeptics have pointed out that Joel almost beat his ride down from the mountain. Regardless, when he came down, he had a plan, an agenda that would challenge all the sects of Mormonism. No one at the time had ever heard anything quite like it from Joel or anyone else. Something happened there.

Ross's Church was a total departure from what the LDS church had become. The ideas he championed would take years and a lot of diligent research and effort to uncover in the LDS archives and journals. Thanks to some of his followers and many anti-Mormons, some of those ideas are now mainstream...sort of.

Anti-Mormons? Yes. Some, such as Jerald and Sandra Tanner spent their life exposing hidden and changed doctrines in the LDS church. Many of their "discoveries" validated what Ross was teaching. Some, such as Ross' rebellious convert Fred Collier, rejected and changed those teachings and inspired some faithful LDS scholars to accept and perpetuate erroneous ideas used to justify "One Man" authority from the fictional "last charge" to the Council of 50 and the equally dubious "Transfiguration of Brigham Young." Since Fred published many of his doctrines, these have somehow become the doctrines of Ross' Church in the public understanding. But they are Fred's, not Ross'.

Ross wasn't about to be subject to his little brother on a program that he felt was wrong. Joel insisted that as the president of the CFBFT, he should be in control of the charter They separated. Joel and Floren returned to Mexico. Ross then chartered The Church of the Firstborn. (CFB) December 1955.

Joel's church (CFBFT) was formally reorganized on April 6, 1956, with Joel at its helm as the First Grand Head of Priesthood (TPJS p.166) and as President. If one does a careful reading of DC 124:123-126, it shows Joel's model. Once you see it, it is easy to believe that it was always there. Hiding in plain sight.

> 123 Verily I say unto you, I now give unto you (Joseph Smith, as first Grand head.) the officers belonging to my Priesthood, that ye may hold the keys thereof, even the Priesthood which is

after the order of Melchizedek, which is after the order of mine Only Begotten Son.

124 First, I give unto you Hyrum Smith to be a patriarch (Second Grand Head.) unto you, to hold the sealing blessings of my church, even the Holy Spirit of promise, whereby ye are sealed up unto the day of redemption, that ye may not fall notwithstanding the hour of temptation that may come upon you.

125 I give unto you my servant Joseph to be a presiding elder (President) over all my church, to be a translator, a revelator, a seer, and prophet.

126 I give unto him (Joseph Smith) for counselors my servant Sidney Rigdon and my servant William Law, that these may constitute a quorum and First Presidency, (Joseph Smith, Sidney Rigdon, and William Law) to receive the oracles for the whole church.

Joel's first action was to call Fundamentalist leader Rulon Allred to become the number two man in his organization (LeBaron J. F., 1955). Rulon, of course, refused the dubious honor. Joel next tried to entice Margarito Batista. Margarito also declined. Interestingly, Joel's Priesthood genealogy for the number two position, which he termed "the second grand head of priesthood," always featured Margarito Batista as the last of the fundamentalist line that originated with John Taylor, the entire line being designated as holding the keys to the office held by Hyrum Smith as the second grand head under Joseph Smith.

Because of Brigham Young, in LDS circles, it is fanatically believed that only one man at a time can preside over the Priesthood. (DC 132:7, parenthetical insertion). Brigham Young misinterpreted and weaponized that idea after Joseph Smith died. In 1918, Charles W. Penrose amplified and codified the idea. He was attempting to disqualify anyone from performing plural marriages. There are serious problems with that interpretation, but no one aspiring to head a Mormon splinter group will ever succeed without claiming to be the "One." Brigham and Penrose did a fantastic job of indoctrinating the LDS church and all the fundamentalists with that idea.

Joel was determined to restore the correct organizational structure and put the house of God in order. His final organization was close to what Joseph Smith accomplished just before his death. It even included a somewhat similar but secret part like his brother Ross was attempting.

For converts from the LDS Church, Joel's interpretation of First Grand head naturally leads to the idea that he was the "one man" at a time. But we must remember that Joel didn't initially claim to be that "one." However, his followers, having been indoctrinated by the LDS church, soon forced it onto him. After he was killed without leaving a designated successor, the idea left his church adrift for at least 40 years.

Chapter Ten - Early Growth of the Church in Mexico and French Missionaries

When Joel organized the CFBFT, it started slow. Ervil joined and devoted his full time and energy to his brother's church. Initially, Ervil's missionary efforts were aimed at converting the Mexicans from southern Mexico. His efforts there borrowed from the teachings of Margarito Bautista. Plural marriage, and United Order. Ervil continued with his desire to publish. Drawing heavily from Musser's two pamphlets, "Priesthood Items" and "A Priesthood Issue," he wove Joel's priesthood claims into a document called Priesthood Expounded. In August of 1956, they published a few thousand copies.

In Chihuahua, one of the early converts was Noel Pratt. He energetically began to publish various tracts and pamphlets. Working together, he and Ervil formulated sixty questions (see Appendix). They felt the questions could not be answered by the various branches of the Mormon church without compromising their own claims to authority. They were incorporated into The Prophet's Challenge, with Joel listed as its author. Joel presented his challenge and assumed authorship of the 60 questions and the supervision of Priesthood Expounded.

Like any religious fanatic, Ervil was willing for his brother to take the credit.

Because many in the LDS church felt that things were out of order, Joel's church began to grow in large part because of the efforts of Noel Pratt and Ervil. By December 1958, Ervil was replaced as President of the Mexican mission by Fernando Castro, who served under Ervil's supervision. Castro was a convert from Bautista's group and was given that responsibility. He would later lead a group that still exists in Baja California.

It seems that Joel and Ervil were truly "Called of God," but there began to be problems.

After two years, Pratt left. He felt that Joel ran too slow with no leadership ability and that Ervil ran too fast. Ervil was converting the poor Mexicans with promises of a United Order as soon as they gathered to the ranch. A process that was bankrupting the church. Pratt maintained that Ervil was covetous and sought authority and political power. Looking at what Pratt accomplished, I personally tend to feel that he also sought authority and power. His efforts were frustrated by Ervil's accomplishments in the south and the acceptance of Priesthood Expounded as the church's primary missionary document.

Explaining what was scripturally and functionally wrong with the LDS church was simple. Fundamentalist groups were also easy to deal with. We need to recognize that most of the early converts already felt that the LDS Church was adrift. The proselyting was primarily a hope-inducing effort. Joel's church promised a return to God's plan and met with success. The Church of the Firstborn of the Fullness of Times grew, Ervil was in time called to assume the office of Second Grand Head. A position that elevated his influence and prestige. Again, we see Joel and Ervil as a unit. A favorite idea at the time was to link the first and second grand heads together historically. Melchizedek and Abraham; Jesus and John the Baptist; Joseph Smith and Hyrum; Joel and Ervil.

Let me reiterate: Most converts were already unhappy with their church. Their conversion was based on hope. Hope for a return to the correct form of worship.

In France, an exceptional missionary named Bill Tucker was destined to upset that mission. William P. Tucker was not born in the church. He converted when he was 15. He had many unresolved questions and immersed himself in a study of church history and doctrine. He completed a graduate degree and planned to enter a Ph.D. program at UCLA. His studies were interrupted because he was called to be a missionary. Being a very devout man, he accepted the call. He was an intellectual and inspired confidence. Upon arrival in France, he was assigned as a companion to David Shore. He and David had similar doubts and questions. Together, they studied, fasted, and prayed. They actively sought spiritual growth. Their efforts began to bear fruit. They began to gather converts and perform baptisms. Attendance at church meetings in their district rose sharply. The overall mission morale at the time was very low. The activities of Shore and Tucker attracted attention mission-wide. Other missionaries learning of their success revived their own hopes for success, and the mission prospered.

Bill soon received a call as councilor to the mission president. This was an honor for any young missionary. It also gave him access to the other French missionaries.

David Shore completed his mission and returned to the states.

The LDS church was trying to get a uniform approach to missionary work and that meant that only certain works and approaches were acceptable. Bill began to "sound out" other missionaries to determine who he could confide in. Soon, many of the missionaries started to study and read some of the "forbidden" publications such as the Journal of Discourses. The French missionaries were holding secret study meetings but were still convinced that the church was right. Just a bit off the path. Bill's efforts offered hope for a correction.

Bill taught the importance of seeking the spirit for guidance in missionary work. Among those that he felt comfortable with, he encouraged them to ignore the current Church leaders 'teachings in favor of "old-time religion" doctrines from the early church. He taught against blind obedience and asked them to study, fast, and pray so they would know for themselves.

Meanwhile, David Shore was in the US searching for answers. He encountered a copy of "Priesthood Expounded." Impressed, he forwarded a copy to Bill Tucker. Bill found it to be very enlightening as it provided answers to some of his questions and doubts. He shared these insights with his trusted missionary companions.

Bill had a great influence over the entire French mission. One estimate was that over one-third of the 130 missionaries serving in France were influenced and in sympathy with his teachings. Others have estimated that at least thirty were firm believers.

Someone reported the situation. When the mission president realized the seriousness of the problem, he asked for help. Apostle Hugh B. Brown was immediately dispatched. At first, he considered just shutting down the mission but, after some consideration, decided to wait until the occasion of the dedication of the London Temple. He then conducted "temple worthiness" interviews with each of the French missionaries. Most repented and were able to continue their mission. Nine were excommunicated. Of these nine, seven converted to the CFBFT. Four men and three women. Bill Tucker,

Steven Silver, Bruce Wakeham, Dan Jordon, Marilyn Lamborn, Juna Abbott, and Nancy Fulk. Later two other French missionaries also joined the CFBFT: David Shore and Thomas Liddiard.

The other two French missionary "apostates" were excommunicated for such insignificant things as being honest about not "knowing" that David O. McKay was a prophet. Hugh B. Brown showed an abundance of faulty judgment or a total lack of discernment and inspiration.

The French mission converts all lived in Mexico for some time and supported the LeBaron movement. Each of the six male French missionaries: Bill Tucker, David Shore, Stephen Silver, Dan Jordan, Thomas Liddiard, and J. Bruce Wakeham were named apostles when Joel fully organized his church.

Marilyn Lamborn and Nancy Fulk married Tucker, the latter union ending in divorce. Juna Abbott married Wakeham. Dan Jordan became a close associate of Ervil LeBaron and was indicted for the murder of Joel LeBaron. David Shore eventually returned to the LDS Church after the death of Joel. Bruce Wakeham attempted to claim to be Joel's successor after the death of Verlan. Steven Silver abandoned the church and his wives for personal reasons not related to church doctrines.

Bill was the only one who questioned the doctrine. Actually, he questioned everything, including God. He is quoted: "If there is a God, Mormonism is true. If Mormonism is true, the LeBarons have the truth". This was shortly before he died. (LeBaron V. , 1981)

I believe Bill's withdrawal had more to do with not receiving a higher office in Joel's church. High expectations that are not realized seem to be powerful emotions that lead to problems. Bill shared this trait with Ben LeBaron. Both were intelligent. Both excelled. Both expected more, and both were disappointed.

With the conversion of the French Missionaries Priesthood Expounded was a success. Ervil's efforts were vindicated, and he became the one in charge of the overall missionary program. Later, he also accepted his appointment as the Second Grand Head of Priesthood.

Chapter Eleven - Rapid Growth and Problems

The growth of the church accelerated after the conversion of the French missionaries. People were converting. They were both mainline LDS and fundamentalist. The doctrine of the gathering was drawing those converts to Colonia LeBaron. It soon became obvious that one important thing wasn't happening. There was no United Order to accommodate the influx of members. Ervil organized one. He drew heavily on the talents of the French missionaries to make it functional. After about two years of effort, it failed. The blame fell squarely on Ervil. He blamed the members. No one blamed Joel.

During the time of Ervil's United Order experiment, Joel was devoting his time to various ventures in the mountains west of Col LeBaron. These were supposed to be economic opportunities for those who invested in them. These investment ventures also failed. It seemed that neither communism nor capitalism worked for the church. Some converts left, but converts were coming faster than they were leaving.

Throughout the ages, people have deified their leaders. The Church of the Firstborn of the Fulness of Times was no exception.

The French missionaries were also the source of much of the hero worship. They searched the standard works and tied Joel to dozens of predictions that were for Christ, Joseph Smith, and others. An example of this is Revelation 11:3-13. The two witnesses that would prophesy a thousand two hundred and threescore days, be killed by the beast, lie in the street for 3 ½ days be resurrected, and ascend into heaven. Joel and Ervil, obviously.

I believe the missionaries may have also been responsible for making Joel that "one man at a time" which caused his church so many problems after his death. His early proclamations were only for the one mighty and strong. Brigham Young had promulgated the one man on the earth at a time using that erroneous interpretation of DC 132:7 (Parenthetical insertion). Penrose had emphasized that interpretation. He used it to restrict the number of people who could authorize plural marriage to the President of the LDS Church. The LDS church members had been totally brainwashed to believe in that interpretation. Of course. Joel had to be that man.

No doubt Joel accepted that interpretation. All the members of the CFBFT did for sure. After Joel's death without a designated successor, this became a major problem. With both Joel and Verlan dead, the church leaders decided they no longer had any priesthood. Not even enough to baptize their own children. This situation existed for more than 40 years.

Joel is often described as humble. He was hard-working, wore work clothes, traveled in 2nd class buses, or drove old cars. This became his badge of honor and led to even more worship.

People went to Joel and Ervil for "divine" council on the pettiest of problems. Many would make no move without the explicit approval of Joel or Ervil. This is where we must place blame on their followers. Freedom from responsibility is more attractive than freedom to choose. People are willing to trade their independence for relief from the burdens of thinking, deciding, and being responsible for their decisions.

Verlan wrote in the LeBaron Story: "Joel was continually besieged with other's problems, often making it impossible to tend to his own business."

> "Some were disappointed at Joel's disinclination to delve into every detail of their business. Others marveled, considering it a sign of wisdom that he left so much to individual choice and discretion. Those who felt a sense of dissatisfaction in his counsel often found that Ervil was full of advice on exact ways and means of doing things."

There is a contradiction there, or maybe a truth. Verlan shows Joel's reluctance to tell or dictate what people should do but also his willingness to hear and perhaps counsel them. People often felt that they had Joel's approval for things they wanted to do. I had a personal experience of how unwilling anyone was to do anything without the explicit approval of Joel. I had been given a job, a calling to act as the bishop's agent/presiding elder in San Diego, Tijuana, and Los Molinos. One day in Los Molinos it was raining and flooding with a lot of water running directly into the building that served as our chapel. Water was pooling at the entrance. I suggested that we dig a small ditch to direct the water away from the building. No one was willing to help me in any way without talking to Joel first, I resigned that calling in Los Molinos as soon as I could.

Such people are ripe candidates for exploitation.

Joel's main error was not actively suppressing their hero worship. Joel perhaps just didn't know how to counter it. Ervil, on the other hand, actively embraced that blind faith and adoration and gave instructions in such a way that he expected compliance with his advice.

This is where we begin to see: "their hearts are set so much upon the things of this world and aspire to the honors of men." Who's at fault? Not just Joel and Ervil. All their followers who chose to follow blindly were the catalyst that budged the leaders into appreciating all those things that success brought to them. Things they had never hoped for when they began.

The CFBFT was getting serious attention from the LDS Church. Several attempts were made to discredit it. The French Missionaries led the effort to answer these attempts, but they weren't the only ones. There was an ex-Catholic priest, several successful businessmen, at least two Mormon Bishops, a member of the FLDS Council of Friends, a prominent artist who was employed by the LDS Church, and an American diplomat. There were many highly educated and influential converts. They all contributed to the successful growth and defense of the church.

Did they all worship Joel and Ervil? In general, Joel yes. Ervil no. But a few worshipped Ervil. Dan Jordon was one of those.

Some of the early LDS attempts to deal with the CFBFT were at best pathetic. Bruce R. McConkie wrote a prime example:

> How to Start a Cult
> or
> Cultism as practiced by the so-called Church of the Firstborn of the Fulness of Times Analyzed, Explained, and Interpreted; as also: Dissected, Divellicated, Whacked up, Smithereened, Mangled, and Decimated
> or

An Essay Showing Where All Good Cultists Go.

Bill' Tucker's reply is worth reading. Here are the first two paragraphs of that reply:

> "It is astounding that one numbered with the leaders of the L.D.S. Church would abase their literary standards and undermine the dignity of his associates by stooping to misrepresentation, misquotation, yellow journalism and character assassination. The very fact that you have employed these treacherous techniques exposes the weakness of your doctrinal position. You dodge the issues. You falsely describe our doctrines. You deliberately misrepresent the testimonies of the dead. You try to cloud or discredit the real doctrinal issues by name-calling and fable reciting. You attempt to undermine truth by slandering its proponents. The lengthy title which expresses your desire to dissect, mangle, etc., the Church of the Firstborn of the Fulness of Times is obviously designed to make up for what

the article lacked – that is, even one substantial point against your priesthood doctrine.

In the doctrines of your proposed cult, THE CHURCH OF EXALTED ANIMALS OF ALL AGES, you have demonstrated a remarkable agility to mix up truth and error, a skill which requires much practice – a skill which is highly developed in some lawyers and clergymen." (Ensign vol 2 -1)

Bill devoted three issues of the Ensign to thoroughly embarrassing McConkie.

It is important for us to note that some of Ben's ideas remained with Ervil. "Milking the Gentiles" became what some fundamentalists call "bleeding the beast".

How can one finance the printing and distribution of those all-important pamphlets? How can a man with multiple wives, and even more multiple children provide for such a large family. The rationalized answer: by "Bleeding the Beast".

Because of the history of persecution and prosecution of Mormon polygamists, there exists a distrust of the government, the LDS church, and society in general. They see the unfairness of the way they have been treated. Taking advantage in turn seems fair. Many use bleeding the beast as an excuse for misusing government services, Ervil was not so narrow in his definition. The Beast was Babylon, the entire nation, even the whole world that opposed God's "true" messengers.

Ervil was totally devoted to his brother's church. In his mind he, as God's messenger, had the right to "bleed" anyone and everyone. It was easy to justify taking advantage of even loyal followers whenever the opportunity presented itself.

Chapter Twelve - About Me

Because I am telling this story from what I consider to be a unique perspective, I feel the need to explain my history.

I have been associated with LeBarons all my life. In 1934, my mother was courted by Ross Wesley LeBaron. They had known each other from the time they lived in Chihuahua as neighbors. In 1935, she chose to marry my father instead.

When I was born in St. George, Utah, my grandmother and her oldest daughter, Annie LeBaron delivered me.

Many of the LeBarons that were associated with my family lived in Mexico. Alma Dayer LeBaron Sr. had been led to raise his family in Mexico. He sincerely believed that it was necessary that his family mix with the Lamanite people. He encouraged his sons to take Lamanite wives and begin this process. Most of them did. Many of the present-day descendants of Dayer are of mixed blood. They believe the hybrid result is a superior individual.

They are bilingual, comfortable in both cultures and recipients of the promises of 3rd Nephi.

Dayer raised his family in The Mormon Colony known as Col. Juarez. It is located close to Casas Grandes and Dublan in the State of Chihuahua. He, however, felt the need to live in a different part of Mexico where his family would not be subject to the ostracism, discrimination, and social domination of the LDS community. He chose an area some 50 miles east of Casas Grandes in the Municipality of Galeana.

He sold his Col. Juarez property, intending to purchase property in an Ejido. Ejidos are a communal type of property. To move there required the approving vote of the Ejido members. This was met with some resistance. Mexicans are wary of accepting Americans into their special "natives only" institutions. There was even the question of whether it was legally possible. So, it took more time than anticipated. Having already sold his Col. Juarez property, he purchased land in El Valle, a non-Ejido farm town that adjoined the desired property. In September of 1944 he transferred his family to El Valle. It would be several months before he was able to join the Galeana Ejido. Once he was able to move there, the land showed promise and soon other family members joined him. Two of those were Cleveland LeBaron and my aunt Annie.

A few years after his release from prison, my grandfather, Isaac Carling Spencer, had a dream. In it he was told to take his family and return to Mexico. He did so. He took up residence just south of the LeBaron ranch in one of the El Valle properties. He lived there until his death.

My mother was a niece of LeRoy Johnson (Uncle Roy), who led the FLDS group for a time and who apparently coined "Keep Sweet". She had brothers and sisters who married into polygamy. One of them, my aunt Lucy, became the third wife of Verlan LeBaron. Another married a Jessop. Some other siblings joined the Allred group. My mother and the rest of her family remained with the LDS church. I was raised as a true-blue Mormon. (TBM)

When I was nine years old, I went to live with my grandmother Lydia in Glendale, Utah. Here I experienced my first interactions with polygamists. My grandmother would work so she could squirrel away food, clothes, blankets, and other items. If her polygamous family came by, it would be like a herd of locusts had hit. Shelves and cupboards were left empty. She would soon be filling them up again. As a child, the one thing I knew for sure: I wasn't going to be a polygamist. What I didn't realize was that my grandmother wanted to be able to help them and was very happy that she could.

In 1949, we almost moved next to the LeBaron ranch. My recently divorced mother accepted an offer to move to Mexico, where we expected to live with my grandfather. We traveled by bus to Mesa, Arizona where we awaited our ride south with Cleveland LeBaron.

When Uncle Cleveland arrived to take us, there were conditions. My mother would have to become Cleveland's third wife. She found that totally unacceptable and said no. We moved instead to Farmington, Utah to live in the home of one of the wives of Owen Allred. In 1949 Owen moved his family to Draper, Utah. We continued to rent the house. An old, two-story farmhouse close to the Centerville line. This is where I met Floren LeBaron. He had a job somewhere close to Farmington, and he boarded with us. He was about 9 years older than me, but he proved to be a friend and a good influence on me.

One of our neighbors was Rhea Kunz, plural wife of Morris Kunz, and the sister of Rulon and Owen Allred. I was present at her home when Charlotte

Kunz announced that she intended to marry Verlan LeBaron. This was not received as good news. Dayer LeBaron had made some claims to authority and had remained apart from the fundamentalist organizations. The crazy antics of Verlan's brother Ben were an embarrassment to the polygamist groups. The LeBaron name was not popular among them.

I have to say that Charlotte must have really loved Verlan to go ahead after all the opposition she received. The opposition must have gone away though. Her half-sister Irene soon followed as Verlan's second wife. My Aunt Lucy became his third.

Living in Farmington was a great adventure. Among my fondest memories was that of picking fruit on shares. A fundamentalist named Carl Jentzsch owned a farm in the mouth of Farmington Canyon. All the kids, 10 or older, in the polygamous families were allowed to pick fruit. Two boxes for Carl, one to take home. But with the opportunity to eat all the fruit and berries we wanted.

Some of you may have read the "poor me" books written by Verlan LeBaron's second wife, Irene (Kunz LeBaron Stubbs) Spencer. In her book Shattered

Dreams, she remembers it as excruciatingly hard work required to support her family. Poor abused child. If she could at least once tell the truth, she would admit she loved it as much as I did. Just take it all with a double dose of salt and remember that her books were written to sell, not to tell the truth.

While living in Farmington my mother married a man from Escalante, Utah. We left Farmington and moved to Escalante. I lost track of the LeBarons and the polygamists while I lived there. The only incident related to them involved a native of Escalante who had boarded with us in Farmington. He decided he was the "One Mighty and Strong." He decided that as the "One Mighty and Strong" he needed to set the church in order. He apparently caught the religion bug from Floren while boarding with us in Farmington. He was the first of dozens of One's Mighty and Strong that I have met. Claiming oneself to be the One Mighty and Strong seems to be a favorite thing among Mormons.

Sometimes a little knowledge of religion is a dangerous thing.

When I was fifteen, I left Escalante to live with my father in Las Vegas. I had a job working in one of the strip hotels. Full time during summers and weekends during high school. Those were simpler times. I just lied about my age and obtained a social security card and a sheriff's card which allowed me to work in a casino. I worked in the kitchen storeroom, but there was gambling in the building.

In 1955, my mother left Escalante. She moved to Salt Lake City seeking medical care for her ailing husband. Unfortunately, the care was inadequate, and he returned to Escalante where he eventually died. She, with four children to support and no hope of employment in Escalante, stayed in Salt Lake City. When I was 17, I went to visit her for a month. She was working in a machine shop in Sandy, Utah. Ross LeBaron owned the shop. Ross was again trying to convince my mother to marry him.

On the first day of my visit, I went with her to work. Ross immediately gave me a job. I learned how to make some little round part on a metal turning lathe.

The Church of the Firstborn was less than a year old. Ross preached to me non-stop. On weekends, he would take us fishing or on other outings. I liked him, but his religious ideas were just a bit advanced for my 17-year-old view of life. He gave me several pamphlets to read. I took them with me and read them.

I finished high school. I joined the Navy. I married in the temple. I was living in Berkeley, California during the early 60's. I was an active member of the local LDS ward.

I expected to make the Navy a career. I was teaching university-level electronic engineering at Treasure Island, a Navy Base located in the bay halfway to San Francisco. I had advanced rapidly, and I looked forward to continuing my career.

Then two things happened to me. First, we found a mistake in a textbook that we used to teach electronics. It was our "Bible" of electronic theory. It was written by Fredrick E Therman, Dean of the College of Electronics and Electricity across the bay at Stanford. It was the final word on anything electronic. It seemed impossible that something in a book could be wrong, especially that book. But it was wrong. Therman excused it, blaming it on one of his graduate assistants rather than admitting that he made a mistake.

I learned an important lesson:

Just because it is in the book does not make it true AND just because a book has errors in it doesn't make the book all wrong.

This had a profound effect on the way I looked at things from that time forward. It was the beginning of a "question everything" attitude for me. It went into all aspects of my life, including my faith. Just because it came from Salt Lake City did not make it right.

Chapter Thirteen - Why I Left the LDS Church

About this time, I was being groomed to advance in the church. I was very active in the ward. I was the 1st councilor to the Elder's Quorum President. I had been a Navy group leader in several locations. I was a Scout Master. I was completely immersed in LDS activity and quite happy about most of it. But I lacked the most essential credential: missionary work. My Bishop got me a Stake Missionary call. I was released from the Elders Quorum Presidency and the Boy Scouts.

I suddenly came face to face with the memorized "Canned Plan", the hard sell for religion. I had already met the hard sell as a salesman. I was very familiar with all the hard sell strategies such as:

- ☐ Get an early commitment.
- ☐ Give them the answer, then ask the question.
- ☐ Compliment them at every opportunity.
- ☐ Give them choices, all of which are yes.

Example: Would you prefer baptism this Saturday, or is Sunday better?

I knew the memorized plan was wrong in concept. It misused scriptures. It was an insult to the intelligence of the investigators. It was modeled after other memorized hard-sell scripts.

It didn't set right with me. Matt 10:19 seemed more appropriate: "Take no thought how or what ye shall speak: for it shall be given you in that same hour what yea shall speak." Yes, I know that scripture wasn't for the missionaries. And yes, I know that Luke 22:35 didn't say without purse or scrip(t). But both of those scriptures had been consistently misused as I grew up in the church. Most Mormons at that time understood them as prohibitions to prepared or memorized talks. Regardless, where was the spirit of revelation? Where was God allowed to interfere with this memorized sales pitch? It was just so wrong in my estimation.

I was an effective missionary. I didn't follow the plan but had more conversions than my missionary companions. They repeatedly tattled on me because I deviated from the plan. I would argue the plan's lack of merit at all our missionary meetings. I found errors in some of the scriptural interpretations. It didn't matter. I had to accept that the thinking was done. It was from Salt Lake City, coming from the seat of the church, so, it had to be right. The leaders of the church blessed it, so it was coming from God. I was wrong, and I needed to comply.

But I didn't.

I rebelled. I protested. I became a real pain at our weekly missionary meetings. Even though I was a good missionary in terms of quota, I protested too much and too loudly. I was so disruptive that they were considering releasing me under less-than-honorable conditions. My Bishop came to my rescue. He invented a crisis in the ward and asked for my honorable release so I could return to the ward and solve the crisis. I returned to a ward calling.

But it was too late.

About that time, the missionaries from the Church of the Firstborn of the Fulness of Times came to our ward. They placed a pamphlet on all the cars in the parking lot. I stepped out of the meeting because of a fussy child and discovered the pamphlets. Like a typical true-blue Mormon, I gathered them up and threw them in the trash. All but one, which I kept. I noticed the name "Church of the Firstborn of the Fulness of Times" and became curious.

I remembered the time I had spent with Ross LeBaron during the summer of 1956. He had done nothing but preach Church of the Firstborn to me. I called and inquired about Ross. They told me that he was not with their group. They told me that Ross had spent too much time in a flying saucer and that he was now devoting all his time to teaching a dog to sing. All the other brothers except Ben and Ross were with their group, that is Joel, Ervil, Alma, Verlan, and Floren LeBaron.

We agreed to talk. I met with the missionaries: David Shore, John Shrewsbury, and Paul Taylor. They not only were aware of the problems I had found with the LDS Church, but they had a long list of things I hadn't even considered. These missionaries traveled without purse or script. They were living by the law of consecration aka United Order. All those things and more. Again, I was already convinced that the LDS church had some serious problems. The CFBFT missionaries offered hope for a restoration of the "true" church.

I began to accompany them to churches where I was unknown and to their discussion meetings. I soon learned how easy it was to confound the LDS missionaries and scriptoriums. They simply did not know what their scriptures said. All they knew was the "party line."

The technique was basically:

"I see you have your scriptures with you. That's great. May I borrow them? Thank you.

Now, would you please read this scripture to me? Very good. Can you explain that to me?"

Of course, the chosen scriptures contradicted church policy. No one could explain. Usually, they would go inside and return with an Elder who could deal with us. When that also failed, they would bear their testimony and retreat. It was so much fun. and so empowering.

I also learned how difficult it was for people to make that enormous leap to leave the church. No matter how convinced they were about the problems in the church and the correctness of what we were showing them, they couldn't do it. The hope we offered wasn't enough for them to leave the security of the church.

I don't recall if I joined the Church of the Firstborn of the Fullness of Times first or if I got kicked out of the LDS church first. The incident that finally sealed my fate was the open house and dedication of the Oakland Temple in November of 1964. I was at the gate to the temple grounds every day passing out pamphlets questioning their policy for granting priesthood, including the Negro Priesthood Ban.

This is one of the items where my beliefs do not match those of the LDS or the fundamentalists. Neither then nor now. I am neither for nor against the negro holding the priesthood. My stand was that ALL priesthood should be given by revelation. I am against ordaining a man, a woman, a 12-year-old, or anyone else based upon race, gender, age, or rules. These should be decisions that are handled by revelation, not rules. God can give the priesthood to anyone that he wants to. My position is that we need to know what God wants. In other words, get revelation on the matter.

People without revelation have rules.

At the temple, they tried to have me arrested or at least told to leave. Anticipating that, I had obtained an advertising permit from the City of Oakland. When I showed it to the police, they went inside and told them that they could not remove me. What I was doing was legal. The police told me not to enter the property, to be careful, and not block traffic. That turned out to be sound advice.

Some members were very angry about my being there. One blonde "trophy type" lady in a Thunderbird convertible tried to run over me as she was leaving. Fortunately. I heard the roar of her car as she sped towards me, and I was able to scramble out of her path. She did have a few choice words for me as she sped by. This was my first real experience with the ugly side of the LDS church.

I received a church summons almost immediately. I didn't bother to go. Shortly afterward, I received notice that I had been excommunicated.

I was happy being an apostate.

The part I didn't like was their unsuccessful attempt to persuade my wife to leave me. That and how they successfully convinced my underage sister that she should leave my home immediately. Both of those actions were against church rules and against civil law in the case of my underage sister. I guess obeying the law of the land is a subjective thing.

My sister soon left the "safety" of the home of the bishop counselor where she had been sent for protection. She returned home to Nevada. About a year later he was released and disciplined for impregnating another girl living in his home. My sister later verified to me that his amorous attempts with her were the reason she left.

Chapter Fourteen - I Joined The Church of the First Born of the Fulness of Times (CFBFT)

I did finally go to Colonia LeBaron, in Mexico and I did join. I was baptized in the pleasantly warm springs near Colonia LeBaron. My wife was baptized in the icy cold waters of Anza Lake in Tilden Park above Berkeley. She must have really loved me. It was so cold.

One of the things that probably contributed to my joining was that after a long trip to Col. LeBaron, a place I had never been to, I found it was populated with old friends, relatives, and associates. Charlotte and Irene Kunz from Farmington. Floren LeBaron who had befriended me when I was ten. My Aunt Lucy, whom I didn't know but with whom I had corresponded during High School. I felt comfortable and welcome. I already knew that the LDS church was in apostasy. Here were people living the true Mormon religion: Law of consecration, Plural Marriage, Law of Adoption, and more.

The Law of Adoption deserves some additional comment. I was baptized, ordained an Elder, and sent to a room to recite a vow that was supposed to adopt me to Joel. It was more like a Danite oath.

Years later, I learned what the adoption ritual was, and it sure wasn't anywhere near the same. This was about the time that Ervil's "United Order" failed so I suspect he invented it.

> "Do you Brother DeWayne Hafen of your own free will and choice desire to take fully upon yourself the name of the Lord Jesus Christ with an unwavering determination to do his will, to keep all his commandments and to serve him with all your heart, might, mind and strength unto the end, that you might become a chosen instrument in his hands in the establishment and upholding of his kingdom upon the earth and prepare yourself to be crowned with glory and eternal life?"

My answer: Yes.

"Repeat after me:"

> "In the name of the Lord Jesus Christ and before the authority of the holy Priesthood, I, DeWayne Hafen, in the most solemn manner call upon God,

angels and these witnesses, to attest that by an oath and covenant that is fixed, immovable and unchangeable, I dedicate and consecrate myself, my time, my talents, and all my possessions together with all other things with which I am blessed, to establish, build up defend and propagate the Kingdom of God from this day forth and forever. In the same determination I solemnly promise to uphold my brethren in this new and everlasting covenant, to strengthen their hand and sustain them in their high and holy callings. I shall ever be diligent in the work of God, determined to serve him at all hazards—willing to do his bidding, suffer opprobrium, endure hardships, and face danger for the testimony of Jesus Christ, with all my heart, might, mind and strength I shall observe the conditions of this oath and abide in this everlasting covenant, counting all earthly things as filth and dross for the excellency of the knowledge of Jesus Christ, being willing to lay my life upon the alter of sacrifice should I become indifferent toward the work of God, should I become irresponsible in upholding and sustaining the laws and officers of his holy Kingdom or the authority of the Holy Priesthood should I willfully and maliciously reveal the secrets of that Priesthood, should I betray the revelations of God, should I betray my brethren in this everlasting covenant; or should I prove a traitor to the government of God, I now ask God, the Eternal Father, in the name of Jesus Christ to let me be cursed and let the hand of vengeance rest upon me; let the evils and reproach of my wickedness be upon my own head; let gloomy darkness and misery encompass me and let me be turned over to the buffetings of Satan, to be destroyed in the flesh, that I may not have further power to bring reproach, sorrows and afflictions upon the saints of God. May God help me to be faithful in all things unto the end and grant me a crown of eternal life at his [right] hand. Even so, Amen."

There are several versions of the Danite oath but this one seems to fit what Ervil had in mind.

"In the name of Jesus Christ, the Son of God, I do covenant and agree to support the first presidency of the Church of Jesus Christ of Latter-day Saints, in all things, RIGHT OR WRONG; I will faithfully guard them and report to them the acts of all men, as far as in my power lies; I will assist in executing all the decrees of the first president, patriarch or president of the twelve; and that I will cause all who speak evil of the presidency, or heads of the church, to die the death of dissenters or apostates, unless they speedily confess and repent, for pestilence, persecution and death shall follow the enemies of Zion. I will be a swift herald of salvation and messenger of peace to the saints, and I will never make known the secret purposes of this society, called the Destroying Angel, my life being the forfeiture in a fire of burning tar and brimstone. So help me God, and keep me steadfast".

Leaving the LDS church was not easy for me. I come from a long line of historically significant Mormons. I was and am very proud of that heritage. Leaving the Church cost me dearly. I lost family associations, as well as many friends. Regardless of the cost, It was something that I had to do. I was prepared to sacrifice all things.

As with most religions, that translated to money and possessions. One's worthiness is measured by the willingness to give to the church. The CFBFT was no exception. Willing to pay the price, I did what any religious fanatic would do. I cashed in my savings and other investments. I gave the cash and other items that I felt would help the church. Being from a military background, I observed what we call the "chain of command". I paid my tithing and other cash offerings to the San Francisco area presiding Elder rather than directly to the leaders or the missionaries.

The presiding Elder for the CFBFT in the Oakland/Berkeley area was a sailor named George.

He was a bit older than me. He had a lovely wife named Margaret. He was soon to take a second wife, Vonda White, a married woman with two children. She would years later become known as one of Ervil's death angels. She spent over 30 years in a California prison for one of the murders attributed to her. She was released in the latter part of 2008. But in 1964, she was simply a very dedicated woman trying to live plural marriage and doing the best that she could, holding a full-time job as a pre-school teacher. Only after work could she come home to be a mother and a sister-wife to Margaret. Because of a custody battle over her children, she fled to Chihuahua where she opened a Montessori-type school. Life as a plural wife was very hard for her because of the thousands of miles distance between her and George. But she believed in what she was doing and persevered. We all loved and admired Vonda.

Our families got to be quite close during the first years of our membership in the CFBFT. We continued to do missionary work with limited success. After about a year of living in Mexico, Vonda became quite sick. My wife Juleen and I journeyed to Chihuahua to bring her home. Not long after we returned, we learned what her problem had been. My wife came down with hepatitis. The rest of us took shots, and apparently, Juleen was the only one that caught it from her.

About two years after I joined the CFBFT, the Navy decided to get some useful service out of us. I was ordered to a Cruiser out of Long Beach, CA. George was ordered to a rocket launching vessel out of San Diego, both of us destined for Vietnam.

I was transferred from Northern California about six months before George. Thanks to my mother-in-law's monetary help, I was able to purchase a house in Buena Park, California prior to my departure.

George was on a tighter schedule, and he didn't really have time to settle his family in San Diego properly. We talked about it and decided it would be a good thing if our wives lived together in our absence. He moved his family in with mine just before I left. The three women: my wife and George's two wives got along just great. The only problem was that George began to fall in love with my wife. They both were good singers, and I'm sure it was a lot of fun. He played the guitar, and they both sang. I knew nothing of this as I was far out in the Pacific.

George was able to stay at my home for a month or so before his ship was due to leave. As the date approached, he decided that desertion was a better option. He left for Ensenada, Mexico. What followed was almost a keystone cop episode.

As the church's agent, Ervil had purchased a large tract of land south of Ensenada. George went up into the hills above that land to hide. Just what the long-term plan was and why he didn't just stay somewhere in Ensenada is still a mystery to me. Since Ervil was involved, I suspected that they had a juvenile concept of hiding in the hills, somewhat like Pancho Villa. When I returned from Vietnam and saw where he had been sent to hide, I certainly lost any respect I had for the intelligence of either of them. It was directly across the street from, and a mile or so up into the hills that overlook a large Mexican Army and Air Force complex. Someone spotted George's campfire and a detachment of soldiers was soon sent to investigate. He is lucky they didn't shoot him as a spy. He was escorted to the border and turned over to American authorities. Having missed ship's movement, he got to fly to Japan to meet his ship in restraints, probably arriving at about the same time that his slow, flat bottomed, ship got there.

George and I both found ourselves in the middle of that war. Him on a very dangerous little LST-type ship constructed of relatively thin metal, loaded to the brim with highly explosive rockets. They were doing up close and personal warfare.

Me? I was on a Cruiser, the flagship, no less. If we were ever in any danger, I missed it. My ship would participate in the war at least one day of each month so we could all draw combat pay. Then, we were off on missions to Hong Kong, or the Philippines, or Japan. Our biggest problem was too much time in port. No sailor can really afford that much time in a foreign port.

I returned to Long Beach several months before George. I truly liked living with my wife and his two. I would take them to the Chief's Club for dinner and introduce them as my three wives just to see what response I would get. I was well-known as a Mormon. A non-drinker who didn't party or patronize prostitutes while in foreign ports. Some knew I was not an LDS Mormon but some sort of fundamentalist, probably believing in polygamy. It was fun and a good experience. It probably helped me to finally decide to try plural marriage. When George returned, they moved to San Diego, CA.

Chapter Fifteen - Plural Marriage

My ship was scheduled for an overhaul at Hunter's Point Naval Shipyard in San Francisco. Just before my ship was to leave, we went to Chihuahua to a Conference. When we were ready to return, we were asked to give a ride to three Mexican women who wanted to go to Baja California. Two of them were married to Verlan LeBaron. The third was a single young woman. All three had border-crossing cards, which allowed them to travel a certain number of miles into the US. I was totally ignorant of the restrictions associated with those cards. When we got to El Centro, California, I turned north towards Los Angeles. When we got to the immigration checkpoint south of Indio, the Border Patrol promptly unloaded the women and got them to confess to being on their way to work in Los Angeles. (Border Patrol tactics were and still are to get people to admit to something, regardless of whether it is true or not). The Border Patrol came out to inform me that they were being deported and that I was in serious trouble.

I got angry. I had not knowingly done anything wrong; I suppose you would call that righteous indignation. I told them what I thought of their interrogation techniques and "confessions." I told them that I lived in Buena Park and that it was my intention to take them all to Baja California. Since I had expected to arrive at the border at a very late hour, I wanted to go home, see my children, and get some sleep before I started the journey south. Since it was all the truth, I guess I convinced them. It probably didn't hurt that I carried a military ID card. I suspect they checked and found out that not only was I a Chief Petty Officer but that I held a top-secret clearance. Not the typical people smuggler. They returned the women to me with the proper papers to make a three-day visit to Buena Park. All of this seems impossible to me now that I know how the Immigration and Border Patrol system works.

It was by then very late. As I drove towards Los Angeles, everyone but me fell asleep. As I drove along with my mind kind of in neutral, I received a very definite vision of exactly what I should do. In my mind, I saw that the single young woman would become my wife. I didn't care for her. She didn't care for me. But I saw what could happen. When we arrived in Buena Park, Verlan's two wives got on the phone and shortly disappeared. They were very happy to be north of the Border Patrol checkpoints.

So much for my intentions to take them south.

The single woman, Rita, wanted to stay in the area as well. What had been shown to me was that we were to go to San Diego and apply for a student visa for her. She would go to school to learn English, stay with my wife in my absence, and seek work in a clothing factory, as she was a skilled seamstress. Again, something that should have been totally impossible. But that is exactly what happened, just as I had been shown. I promptly left for San Francisco. My wife Juleen, and my future wife Rita began the great experiment. They became friends. Rita made clothes for the children. Juleen got her to shed the excess makeup and the clothing that I had judged to be inappropriate. By the time I returned from San Francisco, I had a very pretty, young Mexican woman ready to marry me. The change was amazing. I decided that maybe I did like this woman. Actually, I fell in love. Plural marriage didn't seem like such a bad idea after all.

We decided that before we could get married, we should go to Mexico City to meet her mother. The three of us set out for Mexico City. Like Abraham and Sarah in Egypt, we decided it would be best if my wife were introduced as my sister. After a week or two visit, the three of us started to go back to Buena Park. We thought we had all the answers. We arrived in El Paso, Texas, and applied for a new permit for Rita. The Border Patrol promptly confiscated her crossing card and deported her. We took her to Col. LeBaron and left her with our friend Earl Jensen's family. Juleen and I continued alone to Buena Park.

It seems our marriage plans had hit a bump.

We sent money for Rita to fly to Tijuana, which she did. From there, she went to stay with Verlan LeBaron's family in Ensenada, Baja California. Marriage seemed almost impossible because there was no way we could all live happily ever after in Buena Park. I still had months to do on my military contract. Amazing to me, Rita was still willing to marry me. On March 4, 1967, I became a polygamist. My good wife Juleen agreed to move to Ensenada to be with her. I would stay on in Buena Park until my Military obligation was over. About two months later, I got an early discharge. This was because of time served and the fact that my ship was being transferred to the East Coast. The Government would have had to pay to move me to the East Coast and back again a few months later.

I found myself out of the service early, unprepared, with no idea how I would support my two wives and four children. Fortunately, I found a good job in Anaheim. We still hoped to be able to get papers for Rita and live in Buena Park. After a few months of this, it became obvious that we were not going to get papers for Rita. We decided to sell the house and that I would seek work in San Diego. This was about the time of the closing of the major aerospace plants in San Diego. A good job just wasn't available there.

The job I had while living in Buena Park was testing and troubleshooting the guidance computers for the Minute Man 2 and 3 missiles. The computers weren't very reliable so there was a big backlog of work. Overtime was a requirement for the job. I worked 12 hours a day, 6 or 7 days a week. I could get to Ensenada for about one day every other week, sometimes less. With overtime, the pay was very good. Most of the money went to Ervil via George.

142

Chapter Sixteen - Bill Tucker

It was during this time that Bill Tucker died. If you are to understand the hold Joel and Ervil had on the members of their church, I need to talk about Bill Tucker. He was one of the most intellectual men in the Church of the Firstborn of the Fullness of Times.

He was a major contributor to the CFBFT's periodical named the Ensign. (The LDS liked the name, so they "appropriated" it a few years after the CFBFT ceased publication). Bill's presentation of articles was the best. They were the easiest to understand. Bill was a natural leader. He had been the one who brought about the 1958 French mission defection. He was doing everything that he could to further the work. Everyone just knew that he would be chosen as the President of the Church, or one of the councilors, or at least the president of the twelve apostles when it finally got organized in its fullness.

But he wasn't.

I don't know what happened next, but Bill left the Church. We were told that he left because of his disappointment. He died of natural causes within a very short time after leaving. I found out that he had left the church about the same time that I learned of his death. He was buried in a cemetery called Cypress Gardens, a short distance from where I lived in Buena Park, CA. I was one of the pallbearers who carried his body the hundred yards or so from the chapel to the burial spot.

We understood, or at least were told, that because he was in danger of losing his blessings, the Lord took him. We had been taught that only a person who has known Christ, someone who has had an abundance of his spirit, can become a son of perdition. We were taught that if someone had progressed to the point of having their calling and election made sure, they would be taken by God before they could become a transgressor of that magnitude. Bill seemed to have been saved from becoming a son of perdition. Hopefully, he would come forth in glory as an exalted being.

At least that was the popular narrative we all heard. The Doctrine and Covenants seemed to back up that idea.

> ".... and he or she shall commit any sin or transgression of the new and everlasting covenant, and all manner of blasphemies, and if they commit no

murder where they shed innocent blood, yet they shall come forth in the first resurrection and enter into their exaltation; but they shall be destroyed in the flesh, and shall be delivered unto the buffetings of Satan unto the day of redemption, saith the Lord God." (D&C 132: 26)

This incident had a chilling effect on any dissension in the church. No one was ready to speak out against the leaders after that. Here was a healthy, strong young man in the prime of his life, snuffed out in an instant because he went against the truth that he had been given.

Lesson learned. Don't speak evil of the Lord's anointed. Don't reach out to steady the Ark because God will get you.

I believe that this incident helped to put Ervil and others on the path to believing that they could do no evil, no matter how wrong their actions were. They probably believed that explanation for Bill's death, perhaps even more so than the rest of us did. Also, there was the doctrine that the two grand heads of Priesthood, Joel and Ervil, ruled independently of the vote of the people. In other words, they were chosen by God. They ruled over the priesthood which in turn ruled over the church.

> "The keys of the Priesthood were committed to Joseph, to build up the Kingdom of God on the earth and were not to be taken from him in time or in eternity; but when he was called to preside over the Church, it was by the voice of the people; though he held the keys of the Priesthood, independent of their voice." (A sermon delivered by President B. Young, in the Tabernacle, Great Salt Lake City, April 6, 1853, at the general conference. J of D 1:131)

> "God made Aaron to be the mouthpiece for the children of Israel, and he will make me be God to you in his stead and the elders to be mouth for me; and if you don't like it, you can lump it." Joseph Smith, (TPJS p. 363; (April 8,1844), DHC 6:318-320.)

> "I will be God to this people and if they don't like it, they can lump it"....(Joel LeBaron).

Perhaps you can begin to understand why we all supported these men even when we knew they were doing wrong.

I hope that knowing about Bill Tucker will help you to understand how we could continue to support leaders who we knew had personal faults and who were abusing their position. What is it we are always told in the LDS church? "People make mistakes, but the church is true."

Chapter Seventeen - Reality Begins

There is another persistent idea in Mormonism. A myth that we all believed: "There is no paid clergy. It consists of a lay priesthood of unpaid volunteers." At the lowest level, this is true. It has never been true at the higher levels. The top leaders of the LDS church are all paid well, plus they receive valuable perks.

The early LDS missionaries all found monetary contributions in the mission field. They were expected to send money home for their families and for the support of the church leaders. D&C 84:86 and the rest of the section indicate that the Lord expected those who are converted by the missionaries to support them with food, clothes, and money.

Ervil, who was devoting all his time and efforts to missionary work, was somehow supposed to maintain his families and travel throughout the missions that the CFBFT established. He did that by soliciting donations for various projects. If the project required $5,000, he would use that project to solicit $20,000 or more. Everyone thought that they were supporting some important project. This was true but they were also supporting Ervil. I was soon to experience that.

Within a week after Bill's funeral, I was visited by Ervil. He told me what a hard time Bill's wife was having and that she was about to be evicted from her home. The obvious solution being for me to gift her with my house and allow her to take over the payments. I would lose my equity, but it would be a special blessing to Bill's family. I would be able to live in the garage until I was able to find a job in San Diego and move. Surprisingly, as soon as the papers were signed, Bill's wife wanted me gone. I thought that was an unusually ungrateful attitude on her part, but the papers were signed. I had no legal agreement to stay. I found myself living in my car, sleeping in the trunk, bathing in an irrigation ditch, and shaving in the restroom at work. Years later, I learned that Ervil had sold my equity to Bill's wife's family at the fully appreciated price.

Mrs. Tucker wasn't as ungrateful as I thought. We were both used by Ervil to finance his lifestyle and neither of us realized it.

I was able to visit my family in Ensenada twice a month. On one of those trips, my primary vehicle failed. I was still able to make the trip in my old Rambler, but it was not road-worthy enough to make a trip to Chihuahua. I wanted to go to a conference and was offered a ride from Las Vegas to the conference. I faked an emergency at work and got a few days off. I then took a bus to Vegas. That is where I met a person who will be important to this story. His name was Dean Grover Vest. I had never met him, but by the time we arrived at Col. LeBaron I knew him very well.

Dean was living in sort of a dream world of his own creation. He had apparently served in the Navy. He claimed to have been a member of a "Seal" team. He was supposedly an explosives expert and a trained killer. He said he had spent a week or more in a jungle swamp while severely wounded, which led to a medical discharge. He told me of all his adventures as we traveled the many hours through Arizona, New Mexico, and Texas. To me he seemed to have his movies a bit mixed up. Interesting stories, but probably only existing in his imagination. I never bothered to tell him I had been in the Navy. He had a Navy uniform with him that he wore for the opening session of the conference. He wore it incorrectly. He had some ribbons that were wrong. No Vietnam service medal or purple heart. Just random ribbons he had picked up somewhere. The E-3 rating insignia showed that he possibly made it through boot camp. He didn't bother with a hat or the special scarf/tie that goes with the uniform.

He kept up his war-hero dialog until George Hughes showed up and addressed me with: "How are you doing, Chief?" Vest asked me. "Are you in the Navy? I said yes, I had served 10 years. He avoided me for the duration of the conference. I caught a ride back to Buena Park with someone else.

What is important about this? Ervil believed him.

My good friend George and his family saw a lot more of my family than I did. George even asked Ervil for permission to court my wife. No one asked me.

It also seems that while George was the presiding Elder in San Francisco, he never bothered to reveal the source of most of the funds he was giving to Ervil for the church. I was paying more than my tithing, all through the presiding elder, George. This had gone on for years. I was career military. I obeyed the chain of command. I paid my offerings to the presiding elder and never said anything about it to anyone else.

Somehow Ervil thought George was providing all that money. George somehow found money for a new expensive motorcycle that he rode for fun. Me? I got around in my old Rambler that someone had sold me cheap. George lived in a nice new house that he was buying, while I lived in an old, cheap-to-rent house in Oakland. I outranked George. I was being paid incentive pay three levels higher than my rank, and I only had one family to support. I guess Ervil thought that Vonda was earning lots of money, allowing them to live a higher standard of living and still contribute to the church.

In Ervil's mind, I obviously wasn't paying much to the church. No wonder Ervil felt George deserved my wife and that he, Ervil, deserved my house to make up for all those years of not contributing to the church. It was only right that I be a homeless person, reduced to living in my car and parking at night in Santa Anna Canyon.

I find it amazing how much money and the perception of who has it determines so many things.

I did finally find out about George trying to court my wife. The fool told me and asked me to stop having marital relations with her. It was creating problems for his efforts to seduce her. I had a serious talk with George. I can be very persuasive when I'm that angry. The romance stopped immediately. I then did several things. I quit my job and moved to San Diego, taking a minimum-wage job as a gardener. I continued to live in my car, but I spent much more time in Ensenada. I stopped giving money to George or Ervil.

It seems that women were just something to use as trade objects. George could have my wife in exchange for his continuing support of Ervil. Ervil could have any woman he wanted. He took the wife of Nephi Marston and the wife of George Hughes without notice. Something about being with the man that could guarantee their eternal exaltation. A version of the "rescue" doctrine explained by Brigham Young:

> "If a woman can find a man holding the keys of the priesthood with higher power and authority than her husband, and he is disposed to take her, he can do so,

otherwise she has got to remain where she is." (Brigham Young 8 October 1861 discourse on plural marriage)

Life is sweet though. A few years later, Ervil ended up with George's wife Vonda. Probably because George stopped having so much money to give to Ervil for the church. Years later Vonda told me that George abandoned her, and she proposed to Ervil. Perhaps Anna May, the wife of Nephi Marston had approached Ervil as well. Who knows? I don't.

Ervil used the rescue doctrine as justification for taking the wives of good men. Brigham taught it and used it. He said he learned it from Joseph Smith. I'm inclined to believe that Joseph taught it and "rescued" a few women. Whatever the reason was, the women bought it. Ervil ended up with at least 13 wives and fathered more than 50 children. He also raised many stepchildren.

I repeatedly saw these trades: "I'll give you something you want for something I want and it's ok because I am God's anointed servant." Ervil found that he could trade in women, land, money, church positions and other things, all to his benefit and at the expense of those who supported him. I was one of those who supported him, even though I knew that his actions were wrong. I was so convinced of his calling as God's servant that I ignored his failings. We, that is me and others, are probably as guilty as he is for what followed when he set out to kill everyone that opposed him. We helped to create the monster. He, of course, was not the only one that exercised that level of priestcraft. He is simply the most notorious.

These things are not easy to tell, nor understand, but they are important to show the insidious nature of priestcraft. How it can make a good, God-fearing man like Ervil turn into a tyrant. How can those who are the victims of this priestcraft continue to support that person in the face of all evidence that he is doing wrong. Why?

Some have speculated that if a person gives enough to a cause they become heavily invested and are mentally unable to evaluate the cause critically. This is even if it is failing or is diverted from what the person thought was its purpose. I was heavily invested, emotionally and financially in the CFBFT.

I read a book about that time called "The True Believer". It wasn't very kind to people who follow someone like Joel or Ervil. Many of the author's conclusions I agreed with, some I didn't, but it is worthwhile reading to understand the nature of cults and leader-dominated organizations.

Chapter Eighteen - Money, Women, Greed, and Other Problems

With the help of the French missionaries and many others the CFBFT grew quickly. Yes, people left for various reasons, but the rate of growth far exceeded the rate of leaving. Those who left often contributed to the material wealth of the church. Someone once told me, "If you are going to play with the LeBarons, you need to remember that they get to keep all the marbles." The laws of Mexico and our ignorance of them along with our willingness to sacrifice were a winning formula for the church aka the LeBarons. The church never legally owned anything. Even the American-born LeBarons didn't own anything in Baja. But their Mexican-born children did. There are multiple stories of converts moving to Mexico. Paying for land that had no deed. Building houses and shops. Only to lose their investment when they "apostatized". Even apostasy had a benefit for the LeBarons.

By the late 1960s. The Church of the Firstborn was doing very well. It had many converts. Using "church money," Ervil had managed to acquire several thousand hectares of land between the highway and the beach in Baja. All in Ervil's name, of course. Huge projects were planned. Humanitarian ones and strictly business ones, such as building a private resort and harbor in the salt flats south of Los Molinos. The plan was to build a multi-story beachfront hotel and resort featuring a boat harbor with houses and private piers. It's a beautiful beach, and the project had attracted the attention of investors. People who didn't care about religion but who saw it as a profitable investment opportunity.

But all was not well in Zion. While most of us had willingly given all we owned or acquired to the church, some did not. They needed capital to operate their businesses. For example, one invested in real estate. He would purchase a piece of land and build a large, expensive home. He would then live in it while he built another one to sell. He needed his capital. Another raised thousands of animals and needed to have capital for food and their care. I'm not sure how the others managed to keep their money. There was soon a large wealth inequality among the members.

The ones with the wealth were preparing to invest in the project. But they were very unhappy with Ervil. They were tired of being pushed all the time to give him money. This and Ervil was accumulating a very large family. His wives included daughters of many of the men who felt Ervil had pushed too hard and wives who wanted to marry up in the priesthood. (Leave their husband and marry Ervil or someone else of his choosing.) A meeting of the Standing High Council was called, and they aired their complaints. They stated that Joel needed to put some "frenos" on Ervil. Frenos is a Spanish word that can mean brakes or bridle reigns. They wanted Joel to exercise some control over Ervil's excesses. They hinted that if he couldn't do that, they couldn't support the project. Joel said he would consider what could be done. The next day he came back and announced a "revelation" removing Ervil from all church positions.

I thought that was a strange revelation. Obviously inspired by the possibility of them taking their money and abandoning the project. I felt that Joel could have handled it better. They could have put him on a salary or some type of retainer if it was only his money requests. I suspected that it had more to do with his growing number of wives, especially those who wanted to be "rescued."

Or perhaps it was his "luxurious" lifestyle. Nice looking, tailored clothes, always polished shoes, smooth, unblemished, well-manicured hands, and a Ford Crown Victoria, which he kept in immaculate condition.

They were envious of him owning a Ford? Yes, a Ford!

We need to remember that Evil had devoted his life to serving the church, His brother's church. His release had to be a shock to Ervil. Verlan LeBaron paints a picture of growing problems between Joel and Ervil. While some of this may be true, most of it involved complaints from those who were tired of the constant need for money and, more importantly, his taking of other men's unhappy wives. Ervil's reputation as a predatory polygamist was very impressive. But Joel had always supported his brother. In some cases, simply defending the women's right to exercise their free agency. After all, Joel had married at least one woman who felt he was a better choice than her apparently righteous non-CFBFT husband. One thing is certain: Joel supported the idea that a woman had rights in marriage. He supported the idea that a woman could leave a non-

CFBFT husband and marry a CFBFT man. Not exactly the rescue doctrine, but close. Women's rights are something that often gets lost in a polygamist relationship. Joel did champion a woman's right to choose her husband and her right to change her mind.

Ervil was happy to "recommend" aka dictate or to have visions concerning to whom a woman could marry. His version of "placement" marriage. That horrible doctrine practiced by the FLDS and some others.

According to Marianne T. Watson (Watson, 2007), this idea of "placement" marriage by the priesthood vs. allowing a woman to make her own choices was one of the things that led to the 1950s split in the fundamentalist movement. This resulted in the FLDS 'one-man dictatorship and the more liberal AUB. Musser and Allred opposed the idea. Barlow pushed for it. Batista had practiced total control of marriage. Ervil and Alma had been exposed to the control idea during their time with their brother Ben and subsequently by Bautista. They were both very much in favor of controlled marriages. Joel by nature and policy was more open to the idea of free agency as championed by Musser and Joel's brother Ross Wesley LeBaron.

After the split between Joel and Ervil, I witnessed what psychiatrist Elisabeth Kubler explained in her studies of the loss of a loved one (Kubler-Ross & Kessler, 2005). Ervil loved his brother Joel. His devotion had been demonstrated for years. So of course, he didn't believe it at first when Joel released him. His denial of it led to anger. In the bargaining phase, he questioned if the "revelation" came from God or from some other source. When Joel verified that he was released, he is said to have cried emotionally and became very depressed (LeBaron V. , 1981). He, like others before him, could not rationally deal with their disappointment. He, like his brother Ben, began to be delusional.

Faced with the reality that Joel's decision was final, he grabbed what he felt he could hold on to as a leader. He began releasing officers in the church leadership. This included Joel, whom he now called a fallen prophet. He actively sought to take over the leadership of the church. The problem was no one accepted his releases or his efforts to control the church. He was only successful in gathering a few converts to his cause. Ervil began to publish papers and pamphlets. He also organized, or at least named his new organization: "Church of the First Born of the Lamb of God." Or more simply as the "Church of the Lamb of God."

Years earlier, Joel had organized what he called the Civil Law of God. An organization loosely modeled after what Joseph Smith had done with his Council of Fifty. In both cases these were envisioned as non-religious organizations that would unite all people on a civil basis to guarantee the freedom of every race, religion, or creed. Almost immediately, Ervil had recognized this as a mechanism to force people to recognize the rights of others based upon the 10 commandments. Most of us do not realize that each of the Ten Commandments carries the death penalty for violation.

But Ervil did.

This led him to formulate a plan to convert the world. A plan where force would be used to make people obey the basic commandments. In Mormondom, this is Satan's plan. We began to hear about "Blood Atonement". A concept taught by Brigham Young using his interpretation of a verse in

D&C 132. According to him, there are crimes that cannot be forgiven by the atoning sacrifice of Christ, but which require the shedding of the blood of those guilty of those crimes.

> "This is loving our neighbour (sic) as ourselves; if he needs help, help him; and if he wants salvation and it is necessary to spill his blood on the earth in order that he may be saved, spill it. Any of you who understand the principles of eternity, if you have sinned a sin requiring the shedding of blood, except the sin unto death, would not be satisfied nor rest until your blood should be spilled, that you might gain that salvation you desire. That is the way to love mankind." (Brigham Young. February 8, 1857)

During this time, my wife and I took on the responsibility of caring for an aging woman and her severely handicapped son. Both had joined years before. She had "invested" $40,000 dollars in a failed project. Not a project sponsored by Joel but by one of the leaders of the church. Joel became concerned that somehow Ervil would get a copy of the signed receipt for that money and use it against the church. I was asked to find and get the receipt. I sincerely admired this fine old lady. I asked her what it was all about. She told me: "I know they don't have any money and probably never will. If they are so worried, they can have the receipt." I took it to Joel. but I had trouble justifying it. Only because Joel was protecting the church's reputation concerning a project that he didn't sponsor made it acceptable.

In 1968, Nephi Marston was killed in an auto accident. It was Nephi whose first wife Ervil had "rescued" years earlier. Nephi had remarried and had a wife named Oralia. She had 4 of his children. After Nephi's death and at Ervil's urging Oralia married another member of the church as a second wife. She became pregnant and delivered a boy shortly before his first wife decided to "marry up" in the priesthood. Somehow a fancy home in the United States was more attractive than an adobe one in Mexico. At her husband's request, a hearing was held. Most of the members of that council ruled in favor of her being "rescued" and becoming the second wife of the rich member. I didn't. I felt that she should wait at least six months to allow for some reconciliation, but I was the minority vote.

Her husband was so disappointed because of the lack of understanding or support from the council that he abandoned the church, his second wife Oralia, and his infant son. Oralia moved with her children to a community in San Ysidro, CA. close to the border and got aid for dependent children. She had many church members as neighbors. It seemed that everyone had decided that it was all right to let the government support their wives and children. Both Joel and Ervil had families in that apartment complex. All receiving welfare.

Viva "bleeding the beast."

Oralia had applied for Social Security death benefits for herself and Nephi's children, It had taken some time because she was never legally married to him, so her first check was over $5,000. Oralia had approached my wife about entering my family. We had been good friends before and after Nephi's death. Joel, being aware of this, called me to his apartment and asked me to use my influence to convince her to give that $5,000 to the church. I walked out of Joel's apartment and walked directly to Ervil's and joined his cause. It didn't matter how Ervil had used me for money. I couldn't get past the idea that Joel would consider taking that paltry $5,000 from a widow with five young children.

With Ervil's help, I wrote and published a pamphlet challenging some of Joel's teachings. For the April 1970 Conference I traveled to Chihuahua with Mark Chynoweth. We arrived on Friday. We distributed the pamphlet and discussed it with anyone willing to do so. In my opinion, we were winning in terms of discussions.

On Saturday morning, we passed out pamphlets. I then entered the meeting. I sat down near the back and set up my "boom box" tape recorder and microphone. Joel promptly sent someone to remove me. That simply proved to me that there was something wrong with Joel and his doctrine. If it couldn't even be recorded for later discussion, it was terribly wrong. I left that meeting angry, ready to leave, and never to look back.

Floren LeBaron followed me out of the meeting and put his arm around my shoulder. He told me that what had just happened was wrong but that he couldn't let me leave the meeting with the spirit that I had at that moment. He proposed that I accompany him and Thomas Liddiard on a trip to a town named

Cuauhtemoc situated in the mountains west of the city of Chihuahua. I agreed.

In those days, this was a four-hour trip each way. We first traveled to Chihuahua City. By that time, we had given up on any discussion of religion. We then went west into the mountains. As they drove along, I was basically just watching the countryside as we passed it. It was in this setting that I had an epiphany, i.e., a sudden manifestation of the meaning or essence of something. Without warning, I experienced the most dreadful feeling of remorse and sadness that I have ever felt. I was given to understand that if I continued with Ervil this would be my fate for eternity. I have no concept of the time involved. It might have been a considerable time, or it might have been a microsecond. All I know is that I knew what I had to do, or else!

I turned to Floren and Thomas. I told them both what had happened. They, of course, had felt and witnessed nothing. We continued to Cuauhtemoc. They went into a store and pretended to take care of some business. We returned to Col LeBaron, and during the Sunday meeting I publicly renounced my stand for Ervil and related what had happened to me. Joel's doctrine still had some problems for me, but I was out of Ervil's group.

I was a victim of that old hard sell tactic I learned as a Fuller Brush salesman. "Look at these beautiful brushes. Which one would you choose? The red one or the black one? Or maybe the white one?" Never the option of none. If Ervil was wrong, then Joel was right. The idea that the church itself was wrong was not an option.

What is important here is not that for some reason God grabbed me and pulled me back from a fatal path. What is important is that Floren's actions of love and friendship allowed me to be receptive to that manifestation.

There was another consequence of my joining Ervil. When I told him about Oralia's getting Social Security, he promptly had Nephi's ex-wife apply. She had a marriage certificate and was able to claim not only Nephi's children but also Ervil's that had been born before or shortly after Nephi's death.

By searching out precedents, I was able to find a Supreme Court decision that allowed illegitimate children to claim death benefits. We appealed and

Oralia's four children received that benefit, but she didn't qualify for a widow's benefit.

Chapter Nineteen - Captain Midnight: Money, Cars, Dope, and Guns

Other than letting the social security agency support one of his wives and children, Ervil must have been pressed for money. He no longer had a large number of church members to support him. I did get some insight as to how his new church supported him. It happened like this:

In August of 1970, I married Oralia. I moved her and her children to Las Vegas where I was teaching High School. I took that job during the fall Semester of 1969. I had been certified in California and had taught an evening computer class the previous semester at Southwestern Junior College in Chula Vista, a suburb of San Diego. I loved teaching and a full-time teaching job seemed like a good move.

In the Fall semester of 1970, one of my students came to school offering a small poodle-type dog to anyone who wanted it. I decided that I wanted it as a pet for Oralia's children. I went to his home to get it. I met his father, whose name was John, and we started to talk. He was what we would now call a prepper. He fully expected the Chinese to invade soon, and he was going to be ready. Both the White Horse Prophecy (Penrod, 2010) and Ezra Taft Benson seemingly back him up. Elder Benson said in the October 9th, 1960 LDS General Conference that "there is little doubt that the leaders of Red China view war as inevitable and wait only the propitious moment in which to strike." He had purchased several Nevada mining claims and hidden various items in them. Guns, ammunition, emergency food rations. He even had a couple of small artillery pieces. He was also associated with some of the "minute man" type militias of that time. Talking to him, it soon became obvious that he had met Dean Vest and Ervil. Dean used his own name. Ervil never gave his name, so they just called him Captain Midnight. According to John, Ervil and Dean were actively involved in a car theft ring taking cars and guns to Mexico. They were also interested in the tactics of an Oregon-based antisemitic, white supremacist militia.

Somehow, Dean had gotten into that Oregon militia to the point that he knew enough that he caused the arrest of some of its members. He just couldn't keep his mouth shut. Even though Dean helped to "train" Ervil's gunmen, I suspect that Ervil had no confidence or trust in him. This was why he didn't want him to leave his group and go to where his constantly running mouth would cause Ervil future problems. Not just from the law but from the Oregon militias that might blame him for the damage done by Dean who would surely blame Ervil.

A few years later, I verified that Ervil's gang was supplying the Mexican drug cartel with guns and vehicles in exchange for drugs and cash. They were distributing the drugs in various locations, including Las Vegas.

How did I learn this? In Sally Denton's recent book "The Colony" about the LeBarons, she references me several times (Denton, 2022). She gets every single reference wrong but one: She says I was working with various law enforcement agencies. That is true, but it is something that she shouldn't have known. She doesn't say how she knew or what I did. This is not something that I would have revealed, and I am hesitant to say much about it even now.

During the time Ervil was threatening to kill the President of the United States, I was requested to go to Caborca, Sonora and meet an agent that was imbedded with the cartel. I was to show him where Ervil's main hideout near there was located. There was a giant lack of communication between the agent and the US Government. The agent already knew exactly where it was. Probably he didn't think it was important and was never asked. Ervil's gang was actively dealing with the cartel. Before the war on drugs caused the fracturing of the cartel, most of the drug trade was controlled by the same organization. Ervil's contacts were many, but for sure, he was involved with what became the Sonora cartel, which had a local presence in Caborca.

Chapter Twenty - Ervil Had the Aces, Joel had a Royal Flush, But the Game Was Over

Prior to Joel's death and even with the problem with Ervil, the church was doing very well. But there was a major problem. Using church funds, Ervil had acquired thousands of acres of undeveloped land south of Los Molinos in Baja California.

Again, property law in Mexico at the time: No foreign national can own property within 50 kilometers of any ocean or 100 kilometers of the border. No church could own any real estate, not even church buildings. All of that "church" property was in Ervil, the Mexican's, name. This was a major bargaining chip for Ervil. Ervil could legally remove Joel's followers. He could offer land and resources to those who might support him. But Joel had a solution. Vacant land that is not in production can be invaded by Mexican citizens who will work it communally. They form what is known as an Ejido and can hold the land if they put it into production. It was a constitutionally guaranteed form of land tenancy. For large landowners, it was a form of "use it or lose it."

In 1970, President Luis Echeverria began his term by declaring land reform dead. But in the face of a peasant revolt, he was forced to backtrack and embarked on the biggest land reform program since Cárdenas. Echeverria legalized takeovers of huge private farms, which were turned into new collective ejidos.

Joel seized the opportunity and immediately sent Mexican members of the church as representatives to Mexico City. Their job was to petition the government for that land. When it appeared that they would be successful, he sent Lamanite members to Puebla and other places in the south where they could entice poor, landless members and investigators to come and become members of the Ejido. Then he sent Osman Jones to transport them. With the promise of land, the Lamanite people came by the truckload.

In addition to the resort hotel and boat harbor, there were other more humanitarian projects. For example, we decided that we should find a way to help the poor kids. The urchins. The street kids in Ensenada. These kids normally just begged for a living and were in horrible economic conditions besides being abused by everybody.

We acquired an option on a ranch some distance up into the hills above Ensenada. Beautiful place. It had once been an orphanage. It was ideal. Our plan was to start a school there. We would gather the kids from the streets and he orphanages. House them, feed them, clothe them, and teach them in English. We would also do practical learning. Each child was to learn a trade. We would produce some items for sale. We would get projects for different trades such as assembly and machining contracts. The students would learn by doing, and also earn some money. Their earnings were to be put into a trust fund to be given to them upon graduation. The idea was that they would leave the school with a trade, a command of the English language, some accounting knowledge, plus enough money to get started in business. It was a good idea, and it attracted interested people. Donations, donations, and more donations were available.

I was to be the school's director. I did not renew my teaching contract for that year. I even had teachers who were near retirement volunteering to teach for only an apartment to stay in. Two days after the ejido was approved, Joel was killed. I was in the process of leaving Las Vegas and moving to Ensenada when that happened.

The manner in which he was murdered is probably best recorded in Verlan's *The LeBaron Story:*

> "He then went to the home of Benjamin Zarate where the car had been left. There waiting for Joel, were Gamaliel Rios and Andres Zarate, who had just returned from Los Molinos. Andres told Joel that his parents had moved two days before, and that the house was vacant. As they had the key to Joel's car, it could not be started. Andres offered to go with someone to get the keys. Jeannine left with him in Joel's pickup, taking the others who had come with Joel, while he and his fourteen year old step-son Ivan, stayed to get the car ready. Andres seemed especially friendly and very talkative. Though he had assured Joel that they would be back in just a few minutes, it seemed that the Zarate home was much farther away than had been

expected. Andres was a little vague in giving directions. When asked how much farther they had to go, he assured those with him that they were almost there. As they drove up a steep hill on the north side of the city, the road ended. He told Jeannine to wait there for him and walked out of sight over the Zarate home was much farther away than had been expected. Andres was a little vague in giving directions. When asked how much farther they had to go, he assured those with him that they were almost there. As they drove up a steep hill on the north side of the city, the road ended. He told Jeannine to wait there for him and walked out of sight over the hill. It seemed strange that Andres had not taken them directly to his father's home. When Andres finally returned, he did not have the key; but said his brother Cutberto, who was across town at a swap meet, had them. By now everyone was becoming impatient. Why did Cutberto have the keys when the car had been parked for weeks and he had not been using it? However, they drove to the swap meet where Andres again told them to wait. He disappeared into the crowd. They waited, but he did not return. It became more strange as they waited longer. It had been two hours since they left Joel and Ivan and surely; they would be wondering what happened. In disgust, Jeannine finally decided it was best to go back. When she approached the vacant house a crowd had gathered and people were looking in the windows. Something was wrong! She could not see Ivan or Joel. As she entered the house, she called but no one answered. There was blood all over the floor. Someone said that a tall blond man had been shot. Scarcely able to speak, she asked who had done it. In Spanish someone answered, "Daniel." Another person reaffirmed, "Daniel Jordan." Jeannine hurried to the pickup where she found Kathy wondering what caused the excitement. Jeannine told her to get in the truck fast; they were going to the police station. Something terrible had happened! As Jeannine turned to leave, she was stopped by police. Immediately, she began asking question; but was only told to follow them. As she entered the police headquarters Ivan ran and threw his arms around her sobbing, "They killed Daddy!" When she asked who had done it he answered, "It was Dan." The many questions she wanted to ask had to wait; as Ivan was taken away while she was questioned. After she related how she had been detained by one of Ervil's men, the police seemed kinder. They then told her what happened. Ivan said that after his mother left, he and Joel had started working on the car. Gamaliel told Joel that he wanted to talk with him and they went into the empty house while Ivan sat in the car waiting. The men had only been inside a short time when Ivan looked up and saw Dan Jordan walking toward the car. The windows were covered with a heavy layer of dust. Dan did not look that direction, but went to the house. There through an open window, he shook hands with Joel; then opened the door and went inside. Suddenly Ivan heard raised voices! There was a scuffle and a window broke. Shots were fired and Dan came hurriedly out the front door. Gamaliel jumped out a side window. Both fled. When Ivan entered the house he saw Joel lying dead in a pool of blood." (LeBaron V. , 1981)

Unfortunately, everything stopped. Everybody fled away. No more money. All the people that were going to help and donate disappeared. My perspective job vanished.

The harbor project stopped as well, but it's important to know that these situations existed and that these projects were ongoing at the time Joel was killed.

I was forced to seek work in San Diego.

Chapter Twenty-One - The 1974 Christmas Massacre

Following Joel's death, accusations against Ervil and the suspected assailants were registered with the authorities. Also, substantial cash rewards were offered. Some of his supporters still lived among us. Since as no one knew exactly who was on Ervil's side, there was nothing anyone could do about this situation.

To understand what follows, it is necessary to explain Mexico's version of a law to prevent double jeopardy. If a person is accused of a crime and is caught or turns themselves in, the courts have 72 hours in which to indict them formally. If they cannot do that, the person is released, and all accusations are null and void. The person cannot be recharged. Once indicted, additional evidence is welcome and useful to the prosecution as it strengthens the case. But the evidence available during that critical 72 hours must clear a significant hurdle. The closest analogy to that is of a grand jury determining if sufficient evidence exists to indict a person accused of a serious crime.

In 1973, some of the members of the CFBFT found that they might be able to purchase land in

Nicaragua. This was before Nicaragua became a communist country. During the Easter Vacation, nearly all the male leaders of the Church went to Nicaragua. I did not.

Ervil, being aware of how the law worked and knowing that most of his accusers had left the country, decided to turn himself in. With no one to give testimony, the charges against him would be dropped and he would be free of the problem of hiding from the government and the law. Consequently, he turned himself in to the prosecuting attorney in Ensenada.

There was no one that could give the police much information about the murder or the circumstances surrounding it. There was only a 14-year-old boy who had been in the car outside but who knew little about what had taken place within the house where Joel was murdered. He had heard voices. He had heard shots. He knew who entered and left the house but that was all. Important but inadequate. Ervil was not the one who pulled the trigger, nor was he present at the house that day. They needed evidence that would show that he ordered the killing. They had none.

Ervil expected to go free.

Ervil had been in the habit of visiting with me in Las Vegas. He still had the hope that he could convince me to return to his group. I would feed him, and he could have a bed at no cost. It was still a religious controversy.

The last time he visited me he was furious at Joel for soliciting property for an ejido. The property was his ace in the competition for the members of the church. Since it was all in his name, he could offer titles in exchange for loyalty. Or he could evict those who were living on it. He had convinced himself that it was his property and no one else had a right to it. Joel had committed a criminal act. He said to me that Joel had gone too far, and they would probably have to kill him to get justice. I thought: "You and what bunch of Boy Scouts." I did not believe it. I did not accept it as a valid threat.

I was wrong.

As it turned out, Joel was killed two days after the approval for the Ejido.

I decided that I must present my testimony of that threat, voiced to me by Ervil. The hope being that it would be enough to allow the court to hold him until others who knew what had happened in Ensenada could return from Nicaragua. I went to the prosecuting attorney and volunteered to testify.

Mexico allows the accused to cross-examine their accuser. When I entered the courtroom, the whole setup was a bit strange but made sense. The Judge sat on what looked like an elevated pulpit. Ervil sat at the Judge's left. I sat in front of the judge on the same level as Ervil. We could have touched each other. A translator and a recorder sat to my left. The judge led the questioning, or perhaps he was the prosecuting attorney rather than a judge. I never knew for sure. I was glad that the translator was there because I only spoke rudimentary Spanish, but more importantly, it allowed me to hear the questions twice with time to consider my answers. It also allowed me to hear what the translator said to the judge and know if he correctly relayed my testimony.

I testified against Ervil. I related what had happened in Las Vegas. Ervil never addressed me directly although that was his right. Miraculously, he was held for trial.

Later, I learned that many people claimed they could have testified to similar threats by Ervil or some of his followers, but that day, there was only the 14-year-old boy and me.

Later, the people in Nicaragua returned and brought their testimonies to bear. I was never called back to court for any reason. Ervil was found guilty and sentenced to a jail term. There's no such thing as capital punishment in Mexico. Shortly after that, a higher judge in the state capitol reversed that decision and Ervil was released. I was told that a substantial bribe was involved, but I have no actual knowledge of that. Proving that someone ordered a killing is a difficult task. The proof may not have been sufficient. Then again, Mexico has a history as a corrupt country and judges were regularly bought.

In 1974, I realized that if I wanted to use my military education benefits, I had to do it before they expired. I quit the job that I had as Manager for an electronic assembly plant in Tijuana. I found a job in San Diego. I was fortunate to find one where I could be on the American side of the border so I could attend school at night and on weekends.

In November of 1974, I started my new job. The company had a policy that any employee who did not return the day after a holiday would not be paid for that holiday. This was particularly important the Christmas of 1974. Being a new supervisor, I wanted to set a good example. I felt I had to return. That policy saved my life.

Ervil had decided that I should be what he called "blood atoned" because I had been a traitor to his group. I had publicly renounced him, and I had testified against him resulting in his being held and convicted. His people gathered the materials and made Molotov cocktails. These are basically firebombs. They are gasoline and diesel in a glass bottle with a wick that can be set on fire and thrown.

They came to my house after dark. They tossed the firebombs in all three exits to the house. It was a three-story wooden tower house with a huge water tank on top. It burned very well. When the fire started, people saw the fire and hurried to help. They were thinking that my wife, Virginia, had probably left something in the oven, and it had started a fire. They arrived, spreading the alarm and began to fight the fire. They woke up my wife and her two children and helped them to crawl out of a bedroom window.

There was no such thing as electricity or running water. Water had to be pulled from a deep well and carried to the fire by buckets. After much effort, requiring many people, they had the fire almost under control. That was when Ervil's people started shooting, injuring several people, one fatally. As the people scattered, they shot at them. As the shooters began to leave, they shot at and threw firebombs onto all the houses along their route out of town. A person in one of the houses who didn't even know what was going on, looked out a window and got shot fatally. They continued out of town and were gone. They paused only to place some sheets of plywood across the single-lane dirt road that went up a small arroyo away from the colony. They had prepared the plywood with spike nails poking up.

As soon as the people realized that they could, they piled the injured into cars and attempted to go to the hospital. As the vehicles attempted to leave, they got flat tires, and it took a while for all of that to sort itself out. They got to the hospital and the two severely injured died. That was the Christmas massacre at Los Molinos. Two dead and thirteen wounded.

Figure 5 My House that Gog Burned Down

During the Christmas and New Year vacation of 1980-1981, I was in Houston, TX. I was in a mall on the west side of Houston. I came around a corner and there was Duane and Mark Chynoweth. Mark spoke first: "DeWayne, how are you? We aren't with Ervil anymore. We'd like to talk to you". I replied: "OK, let's find some public place and we'll do that". I didn't know if I trusted them or not. We went into a cafe. I sat with my back to a wall. Soon their mother showed up. They reassured me that they were no longer with Ervil. They told me: "You were the intended victim that night, but you never came out." They thought I had somehow stayed hidden inside or that they might have made a mistake in my schedule. They asked what had happened to me. I told them I wasn't there. That I had left in a different car than the one parked by the house.

Until that moment, I didn't know. I didn't suspect it. I never even considered that I was the intended target. The one they wanted to shoot the most. After talking to them, I became very aware. That was the reason they waited so long to begin to start shooting. They waited while my wife and children crawled out the window. They waited and waited until the fire was almost under control before they started to shoot. Once they started to shoot, everyone attempted to run away. The flames got high again. With no one to shoot at, the gunmen left town quickly but fired shots into houses and threw firebombs on their route out of town.

My house was destroyed. They also firebombed two empty trailers nearby that also belonged to me. The only houses and trailers that were destroyed that night were mine. Others were torched, but the inhabitants quickly put them out. One additional person was shot when he looked out a window to see what was happening.

There was a lot of speculation that they had hoped that Verlan Lebaron would come to help put out the fire. Pure nonsense. They knew Verlan was not in town. They knew that he was on a trip to Nicaragua. We and they were so mixed among families. They knew I was in town, but they didn't know that I had to leave. Everything then made sense as to why they waited so long to begin shooting. They thought I was going to come out and I never did.

In "The LeBaron Story" Verlan LeBaron states:

> "The Los Molinos raid had been organized with my death in mind. Ervil told his men that he had received a revelation that I would be there at the time of the attack, and that I would be killed. The Church of the Firstborn would then fall into his hands. He took special care to make sure I would be killed; which explained the many fire bombs and extra gun fire into my homes. He then told his men that it was necessary

to go back; and completely destroy Los Molinos within thirty days, or "the purposes of God would be frustrated." The presence of soldiers, however, seemed to have done something toward thwarting that plan. Having failed to get me at Los Molinos; Ervil immediately set about forming other designs." (LeBaron V., 1981)

Verlan attributes that idea to a conversation he had with one of Ervil's repentant gunmen who wasn't there. I would have no problem accepting that story, except some of the known facts do not align. I got my version from two of the perpetrators that afternoon in Houston. Verlan exaggerates the extent of firebombing and gunfire aimed at his homes. They received the same attention as all the houses that lined their escape route. There was only one house destroyed in that raid and that was mine. Two empty trailers were burned as well. Both belonged to me.

Because the original difficulty was supposedly a doctrinal dispute that erupted within a small group, many families were divided with members in one group or the other. Ervil's followers still lived in the town even after Joel's murder. As Verlan points out a paragraph or so earlier, they seemed to know whenever he was in town and would be looking for him within hours. They knew he wasn't in town that night. They also knew that it was my night to be in the wooden tower house. The car I had arrived in was parked there. Things that didn't make sense before became clear when I realized they thought I was there.

Phone service at that time was very limited. I was at work the next day when, shortly before noon, I received a call. I immediately informed my boss that I was leaving and drove to Los Molinos. The whole place was locked down with soldiers everywhere. After checking on my family and seeing my burned house, I returned to San Diego. By the time I was back in San Diego, the fire and shootings were national news. According to them, it was a battle between rival Mormon polygamous gangs. We were all "raising turkeys on weekends". Whatever that was supposed to mean.

Not only was the news wrong. It was ridiculous.

I went to the offices of the San Diego Union newspaper and asked to see the reporter responsible for the article in their paper. She agreed to see me. I told her she needed to go with me and see for herself so she could correct the errors. She agreed. She and a photographer traveled with me to Los Molinos. She saw the disaster. She interviewed some of the victims. When we returned to San Diego, she published a very true and helpful version of what had happened. The other news services picked up the story, and it changed from a battle between out-of-control polygamists to a true story of murder and arson perpetuated by Ervil's gang.

Because I had started a night and weekend MBA course, I had planned to move my family to San Diego. As soon as we could all leave without seeming chicken, I did exactly that. Upon completion of that course, I traveled to New Orleans to become an area manager. I wouldn't get back to the Ejido for a while.

Los Molinos became Ejido Zarahembla, Intentionally misspelled to avoid government censure of the religious name. Three Ejidos were formed from the "church" land that had been in Ervil's name. There was even some land that was particularly undesirable that was still in his name in 2007. A few years ago, one of Joel's sons thought he could still put together the hotel and boat harbor. He bought up many of the rights to that area before he realized that the whole beach area was environmentally off-limits, with several endangered species. He could do nothing there of a commercial nature.

I eventually moved back there. In the 1980's, I bought several lots there. Today, I own nothing there, but several of my Mexican-born children do. I'm still a foreigner.

After going on his well-publicized reign of terror, Ervil was captured in Mexico and delivered to the US. He was tried and convicted of ordering the murder of Rulon Allred and sentenced to life in prison by the state of Utah. But the killings continued. In 1981, Ervil was found dead in his cell. The first report was that he had somehow managed to strangle himself. Later, his death was listed as a heart attack. Two days later, Verlan died in an automobile crash in Mexico.

That first report said his automobile was riddled with bullets. Some attributed that to Ervil's followers.

I know I said I wouldn't, but I am going to indulge in a bit of speculation. I suspect that both were killed by the government of the US and/or Mexico so they could bring an end to the killings and chaos. Killing them both seemed like an equitable solution.

But it wasn't the end of the killings.

It took many years and many more murders involving Ervil's followers murdering other Ervil followers. Months before he died, he had prepared a list where he condemned those in his group that he felt needed to die.

About the government's role in Ervil and Verlan's deaths: I believe our government wouldn't do a thing like that. Of course, I also believe that Jeffrey Epstein died of suicide. And all of those people just keep falling out of windows in Russia.

Sure, I believe those things.

Epilogue – Going Forward

I have no doubt that Ervil was initially a very good man. He sacrificed his goals in life to further the aims of God and the church.

I also have no doubt that God was with him and with Joel initially. What happened?

There is a propensity for mental illness in the LeBaron family. It existed in both Ervil's father's family and his mother's. But his brother Ben thinking he is the One Mighty and Strong is one thing. Doing one hundred pushups in the middle of State Street in Salt Lake City to prove it is humorous, perhaps pathetic. But Ervil went way beyond that.

There is no doubt Ervil was insane towards the end of his life. He did cause the death of 30 plus people. He is said to have planned first to wipe out the Church of the Firstborn then he would move on to the Kingston group and other Fundamentalists before destroying the Mormon Church. The United States would be taken over as a great step toward world domination.

That takes insanity to a whole new level.

We need to look at the trauma that brought these crazy ideas to Ervil.

I am convinced that his unexpected rejection by his brother was the trigger. He was already primed to believe he could do no wrong. For that we need to look at how we, his followers, helped him to believe that.

There is a well-documented pattern for this. We see it repeated again and again. We see it in religion, politics, even entertainment. Someone will acquire followers. They may be a singer, a politician, an evangelist, or something else. Their followers adore them. They seek ways to be in their presence and hang on to their every word. This leaves their followers open for exploitation.

Somehow being a religious minister can mean big money. Most, if not all, measure their success by how full the collection plate is. Politicians and preachers may begin poor, but they all become rich.

People, in general, tend to deify their leaders. Women tend to be attracted to the alpha male. These tendencies can easily lead to abuse.

With all that attraction and adoration going on it is very difficult for any leader to avoid a trap. Our leaders find they like the things of the world. We are so happy to give them all things, including our trust and loyalty because we honor and worship them so much.

Both Ervil and Joel fell into that trap. Maybe intentionally in Ervil's case. Maybe without realizing it in Joel's, but certainly not actively preventing it. Either way, it is addictive and hard to avoid.

So, who should we blame? Should we blame them for aspiring to these things? Or should we blame ourselves? I'm going to opt for blaming ourselves.

Let us take a well-documented tyrant, for example, Warren Jeffs of the FLDS. He totally abused his followers. In his case, he did it intentionally. His father and others had prepared the FLDS members. They had established the one-man rule. They had rejected John Taylor's 1886 revelation because it allowed men to use their own agency in the matter of plural marriage. They had established placement marriage. The members of the FLDS had already surrendered their integrity and lost the ability to think or challenge their leader. After all, he held the keys to all blessings. He was God's representative on earth. Being an opportunistic predator, Jeffs sought and seized the leadership, and no one stood up to oppose him.

I think we know the results.

I had several relatives living in Colorado City at the height of the FLDS insanity. I couldn't even visit them or correspond with them. It was simply "Follow the Prophet". To them, it was a test of faith to comply with Warren Jeffs 'totally insane and abusive mandates. As an outsider looking in, it was pathetic. I was just as pathetic following Ervil.

Like that proverbial frog in the cook pot, no one is ready to jump out until it is too late.

We live in a nation that is completely dominated by out-of-control politicians. Our elected representatives are totally dominated by their party leaders. Neither we nor they can challenge those leaders. Both sides are totally corrupt, but we emotionally support them. Many of us are ready to fight, maybe die to defend them. Why? Because they have learned just where to touch our buttons.

Ervil learned which buttons were most useful to control his followers. They probably believed that they were doing God's will. Mormon theology provides some very interesting "Buttons".

One interesting "button" is the idea of having our calling and election made sure. This comes from a phrase in the Bible, specifically 2 Peter 1-10. It is widely understood that if we are faithful and diligent in our faith and obedience to God, we can be sure of our salvation and avoid falling into sin.

Mormon theology takes it much further. Having our calling and election made sure involves a specific ritual known as the second anointing where men and women are put under covenant to be willing to sacrifice all things. If they do that, they are promised that they will become Gods.

The mortal person holding the "keys" to this special blessing is that "one" man.

> "And verily I say unto you, that the conditions of this law are these: All covenants, contracts, bonds, obligations, oaths, vows, performances, connections, associations, or expectations, that are not made and entered into and sealed by the Holy Spirit of promise, of him who is anointed, both as well for time and for all eternity, and that too most holy, by revelation and commandment through

the medium of mine anointed, whom I have appointed on the earth to hold this power (and I have appointed unto my servant Joseph to hold this power in the last days, and there is never but one on the earth at a time on whom this power and the keys of this priesthood are conferred), are of no efficacy, virtue, or force in and after the resurrection from the dead; for all contracts that are not made unto this end have an end when men are dead." (DC 132: 7)

The parenthetical insertion is constantly misinterpreted. But it is the favorite scripture for all the scores of "one man on the earth at a time" claimants.

Joel claimed it, Ervil claimed it, Warren Jeffs claims it. Dozens of others claim it. It is the key to power. It facilitates abuse.

Vonda White was sure that she was ensuring her "Calling and Election" by obeying the order to kill Dean Vest. So were the others.

Once Ervil's followers accepted that he was the "one man," they conceded that he had that power and needed to be obeyed. That was also true for the followers of Warren Jeffs and Joel LeBaron. No wonder they all claimed that power. Even if a Mormon leader doesn't actively claim it, most of their followers believe it anyway. That makes it easy to put their brain in neutral, surrender their integrity, and charge ahead. Because their leader has spoken, they are relieved of the responsibility for their actions. Eric Hoffer loved to analyze this aspect of what makes a "True Believer".

The idea is that our leaders receive revelation to guide us. God is in charge, so don't question those revelations. Ervil no doubt was receiving visions. But from where? Certainly not from God. Perhaps from his own mind. Possibly from the Devil himself.

Demonic Possession? I didn't say that. But?

But if we are going to accept and believe that people can have revelations, that God can inspire them, then we must also accept that these things can come from other places.

I have related that people saw and knew things that they couldn't know. Alma Dayer LeBaron Sr. saw the possibility of good soil and ample water at the site he chose for Col. LeBaron. The rest of the

Galeana Ejido on that side of the river is alkaline soil with horrible water prospects. As it turns out, Col LeBaron has good soil with lots of good water. Col LeBaron sits on a major aquifer. After years of farming there, after many good wells, and after modern hydrology explorations, we know that he was right. How could Dayer have known that?

I come from a long line of such visionaries. My great-grandmother recorded things in her daily journal that she could not have known, but which proved to be true. Things like deaths in the family. Others kept records questioning her visions of things she couldn't have known. Later requiring an admission that she somehow knew.

When I was living with my grandmother, one morning she announced to me that her son, my uncle had died. There was no way she could have known. He was in a remote location in another State on a fishing trip. There was only one party-line type phone in the town where we lived. It was three days later when we received that call. But she and my uncle's dog were already in mourning. The dog refused to eat and died shortly after. How did they know?

I have seen things that I couldn't have, but which later proved to be true. Many of them are mundane things that I'm sure God would not have bothered with. This is a worldwide phenomenon. It has no viable connection with being a God sent vision although many of us attribute all such these things to God.

Having been raised a Mormon, I was thoroughly indoctrinated with the idea of "follow the prophet." After the death of Joel, Ervil, and Verlan I witnessed the squabbles among the LeBarons to determine which ones owned the "church" properties. It turned out that the church owned nothing. Everything was the personal property of a LeBaron.

I left in disgust.

I like to believe that if Joel had lived it would have been different. Of course, I will never know that.

I went in search of those magic keys. All I found was other "one man" key holders who were busily abusing their compliant followers.

I gave up.

One day I was given a ride to Oregon. I had the opportunity to visit Carl Jentzsch. The man who owned that fruit orchard in Farmington, Utah. The man who met Joel when he came down from the mountain so quickly to his farm. I asked him if he had any ideas about where I could find them. He didn't. He didn't claim them, nor did he have any idea if anyone had them. He did relate a story that is worth repeating:

He said that he was one of the many polygamists arrested and imprisoned after a raid in 1944. The State offered release if the men would sign papers renouncing the practice. Most of the leaders did so and went free.

Carl said he couldn't feel good about doing that. He didn't know what to do. His priesthood leaders had signed and encouraged him to do the same. Still, he resisted. He related to me that one night he had a vision. In the vision, a messenger came for him, and they left the prison. They traveled to a location he described as a flat field or plain with a large building on it. When they got closer to it, he could see it was a prison. They went in and everyone was dressed in prison garb. He soon realized that the prisoners were past leaders of the church and the fundamentalist movement. He asked the messenger: "Why were these men in this prison?" He had thought they would be on a throne in heaven. Not in some sort of spirit prison.

The messenger said: "They were called of God, but they lost their integrity. Read in the Doctrine and Covenants section 121:34-46 and you will understand."

"34 Behold, there are many called, but few are chosen. And why are they not chosen?
35 Because their hearts are set so much upon the things of this world, and aspire to the honors of men, that they do not learn this one lesson÷
36 That the rights of the priesthood are inseparably connected with the powers of heaven, and that the powers of heaven cannot be controlled nor handled only upon the principles of righteousness.
37 That they may be conferred upon us, it is true; but when we undertake to cover our sins, or to gratify our pride, our vain ambition, or to exercise control or dominion or compulsion upon the souls of the children of men, in any degree of unrighteousness, behold, the heavens

withdraw themselves; the Spirit of the Lord is grieved; and when it is withdrawn, Amen to the priesthood or the authority of that man.

38 Behold, ere he is aware, he is left unto himself, to kick against the pricks, to persecute the saints, and to fight against God.

39 We have learned by sad experience that it is the nature and disposition of almost all men, as soon as they get a little authority, as they suppose, they will immediately begin to exercise unrighteous dominion. 40 Hence many are called, but few are chosen.

41 No power or influence can or ought to be maintained by virtue of the priesthood, only by persuasion, by long-suffering, by gentleness and meekness, and by love unfeigned;

42 By kindness, and pure knowledge, which shall greatly enlarge the soul without hypocrisy, and without guile

43 Reproving betimes with sharpness, when moved upon by the Holy Ghost;

and then showing forth afterwards an increase of love toward him whom thou hast reproved, lest he esteem thee to be his enemy;

44 That he may know that thy faithfulness is stronger than the cords of death.

45 Let thy bowels also be full of charity towards all men, and to the household of faith, and let virtue garnish thy thoughts unceasingly; then shall thy confidence wax strong in the presence of God; and the doctrine of the priesthood shall distil upon thy soul as the dews from heaven.

46 The Holy Ghost shall be thy constant companion, and thy scepter an unchanging scepter of righteousness and truth; and thy dominion shall be an everlasting dominion, and without compulsory means it shall flow unto thee forever and ever.

Carl said to me: "Do you see it? Those men were called by God. They were good men, but they lost their integrity. That is why they were so right when they started, but also why they became so wrong.

They violated the provisions of this scripture. Memorize that part of section 121 and use it to measure and determine who is following God and who isn't."

I have found this to be the best advice I ever got for knowing a true prophet from a false or fallen one. If I had a thesis for this book it would be DC 121: 34-46

If we learn this and fiercely defend our right to free agency, we will not fall victim, nor will we enable these so-called prophets of God.

We will maintain our own integrity and may help them to maintain theirs as well.

I have told of many visions. They were both my personal ones and those of others. If we accept that someone can receive a vision, why don't we realize that the source of that revelation might be God, Satan, or the desires of that person?

Our agency is our most valuable possession. As Mormons, we have been taught that there was a war in heaven over agency. We are taught that our older brother, Jesus Christ was willing to come here and show us the way but that we would have to choose to follow that path. If we stumbled, he would satisfy the demands of justice through his sacrifice. This would be his gift to us. If we chose not to follow him, we would be lost and would not have a claim on salvation. Our choice. Our responsibility.

We also are told that Satan had another plan. He would force us to obey all of God's commandments. No one would be lost. We chose the Savior's plan.

If we value our right to free agency, why are we so quick to surrender it to our leaders?

Why can't we approach God ourselves instead of expecting our spiritual leader to do it for us? I have only met one spiritual leader who refused to do my thinking for me. After asking for his advice on a difficult decision he said to me: "What is wrong with your knees? Can't you bend them enough to get down on them and ask God for yourself? Are you afraid to take responsibility for your actions?"

I think he knew how to avoid the trap that so many have fallen into. And by then, I understood.

Do you understand?

Notes and References

Bronson, J., LeBaron, B. T., Spencer, M., Allred, L., Bronson, R., & Larry, E. (1958). Regarding the Lebaron Beginnings. (C. Bronson, Interviewer)

Committee on Privileges and Elections. (1905, January). Testimony of Important Witnesses. Salt Lake Tribune Publishing Company.

Denton, S. (2022). *The Colony: Faith and Blood in a Promised Land.* Liveright.

Johnson Family Files. (n.d.).

Kubler-Ross, E., & Kessler, D. (2005). *On Grief and Grieving: Finding the Meaning of Grief Through the Five Stages of Loss.* Scribner.

LeBaron, J. F. (1955). Revelation to Rulon Allred. In Author's Possession.

LeBaron, V. (1981). The LeBaron Story. Keels & Co Inc. .

Penrod, D. L. (2010). Edwin Rushton as the Source of the White Horse Prophecy. *BYU Studies, 49*(3), 75-131. Retrieved from BYU Sudies: https://byustudies.byu.edu/article/edwin-rushton-as-the-source-of-the-white-horse-prophecy/

Pratt, L. (1995, August). *Profile of Harold Wilcken Pratt.* Retrieved from Jared Pratt Family Association.

Pulido, E. E. (2020). *The Spiritual Evolution of Margarito Bautista: Mexican Mormon*

Evangelizer, Polygamist Dissident, and Utopian Founder 1878-1961. Oxford University Press.

Quinn, M. D. (1985). LDS Church Authority and the New Plural Marriage 1890-1904. *Dialogue: A Journal of Mormon Thought*.

Schmal, J. P. (2019). *Mexico: Confrontation Between Church and State Indigenous Mexico*.

Singer, M. (1979). Nathan Baldwin, Utah Inventor and Patron of the Fundamentalist Movement. *Utah Historical Quarterly, 47*(1), 51.

The Joseph Smith Papers. (n.d.). *Nauvoo Relief Society Minute Book*. Retrieved from The Joseph Smith Papers: https://www.josephsmithpapers.org/paper-summary/nauvoo-relief-society-minute-book/1

Tullis, F. L. (2018). *Martyrs in Mexico: A Mormon Story of Revolution and Redemption*. Brigham Young University.

Tullis, F. L., & Hernandez, E. (1987). Mormons in Mexico: Leadership, Nationaism, and the Case of the Third Convention. In *Orson Pratt Brown: Life, Times, Family*.

Watson, M. (2007). The 1948 Secret Marriage of Louis J. Barlow: Origins of FLDS Placement Marriage. *Dialogue: A Journal of Mormon Though*.

APPENDIX I - Ordination of Margarito Bautista

Ordination of Margarito Bautista which delegated all the authority possessed by Rulon Allred and Joseph Musser

By Rulon C. Allred June 22, 1951:

> "Brother Margarito Bautista: In the name of Jesus Christ and by the authority of the Holy Priesthood, and by the authority which we hold; we, your brothers, place our hands on your head and we ordain you an Apostle of the Lord Jesus and a Patriarch, and we confirm on you all the authority of the Holy Priesthood which we, ourselves, possess. This we do, so that you may glorify God and for no mean or impure reasons; because if you use this power and authority unrighteously, it will turn to your condemnation by virtue of your holy priesthood.
>
> You are over the Latin American people to continue the fullness of the gospel and the ordinances among them, without having to depend on any other man.

These blessings we confer upon you in the name of our Lord Jesus Christ. Amen"

Ratification of the ordination by President Joseph W. Musser:

"Dear brother Bautista: As a man who holds the keys of the Holy Apostolic Order over the people I confirm on your head the blessings which you have received from brother Allred, and seal on you all the authority which I myself possess. You are an Apostle of the Lord Jesus and a Patriarch, and we give these blessings to you in the name of Jesus Christ, Amen."

APPENDIX II - 60 Questions
THE PROPHET'S CHALLENGE

When Elijah appeared after the three and one-half years of famine, he summoned the priests of Baal to a contest on a high mountain to decide who was on the side of the Lord and who was in possession of divine authority. The contest at that time was to see who could bring down fire from Heaven, as a sign to the people that they might know whom to follow.

The same God who sent Elijah to a contest with the priests of Baal has sent me to a contest with the priests of Mormondom. The contest this time is based on pure knowledge of the Priesthood of God.

I have prepared a list of questions which I call upon all the combined priests of Mormondom to answer. I care not whether my opponents come forth 450 strong, or whether they come forth 450,000 strong. If any of my opposers can answer these questions consistently and in harmony with the four standard works of the Church and the teachings of the Prophet Joseph Smith, without overthrowing their own claims as pertaining to the highest Priesthood authority, I will forever surrender my claims as to holding the Priesthood sceptre and the office Moses held.

But if none among all the hosts of Mormondom can do this — and I am able to answer these questions in accordance with the four standards works and the teachings of Joseph Smith the Prophet — and do so without overthrowing my claims to the highest Priesthood office, I will expect every true man who desires to do the will of God, and is able to understand these things, and who cares anything about the advancement of the Kingdom of God on earth, to step forth, support the work that I have been sent to do, and uphold the authority that has been conferred upon me.

Therefore, I say, let every man and woman examine the fruits of those who are pretending to be apostles and prophets — for the Prophet Joseph Smith said:

The servants of God teach nothing but the principles of eternal life, and by their works ye shall know them. * * * I warn all of you to look out whom you are going after. (TPJS p. 367)

Joel F. LeBaron

QUESTIONS ON PRIESTHOOD

THE SECOND PRIESTHOOD

1. Is the office of the Presiding Patriarch a self-perpetuating office?

2. Who holds the Patriarchal office today that was instituted in the days of Adam and confirmed to be handed down from father to son?

3. Did Aaron hold a self-perpetuating office?

4. How did the Kingdom of God continue in power until the time of John the Baptist?

5. How was the Priesthood office Aaron held perpetuated from the time of his death to the time of John the Baptist?

6. Who is the priest after the order of Aaron today — and through what line did he receive his authority?

7. What must a man receive who is called and ordained even as Aaron?

8. s the office of Presiding Bishop a self-perpetuating office?

9. Is the office of President of the Church a self-perpetuating office?

10. Are there any self-perpetuating offices in the Church of Jesus Christ of Latter-day Saints?

11. Upon what basis did John the Baptist hold the keys of power?

12. By what authority did John the Baptist wrest the keys, the kingdom, the power and the glory from the Jews?

13. What did the Jews lose when John the Baptist wrested the Kingdom from them?

14. Did John the Baptist hold the keys of power and the Kingdom of God in his hands without holding the Melchizedek Priesthood?

15. Can bishops be properly ordained other than through the authority of the presidency of the Melchizedek Priesthood?

16. Were the bishops between the time of Moses and the time of Christ ordained without the authority of the Melchizedek Priesthood?

17. Were men ordained to the Priesthood during that time without receiving the gift of the Holy Ghost?

18. Who was the Elias who appeared on the Mount of Transfiguration?

19. What keys or authority did Peter, James and John hold as a quorum that John the Baptist did not hold single-handed?

20. Was John the Baptist the last of the ancient prophets to hold the authority he restored on May 15, 1829?

21. When Peter, James and John delivered the keys to Joseph Smith, by virtue of what priesthood office did he hold them single-handed?

22. Of what do the keys of organization consist?

23. Of what do the keys of salvation consist?

24. By what authority and in what Priesthood capacity did Joseph Smith the Prophet stand as Prophet, Seer, and Revelator to the human family before the First Presidency of the Church was organized?

25. When John the Baptist ordained Joseph Smith to a priest after the order of Aaron and to hold the keys of this priesthood, what priesthood office did the Prophet receive?

THE FIRST PRIESTHOOD

26. Of what does the Order of Enoch consist?

27. Can the full and complete Order of Enoch exist without a man holding the office and authority Enoch held?

28. Can a man receive the authority Enoch held through a man or group of men who do not hold it?

29. Does the President of the Church of Jesus Christ of Latter-day Saints today hold the Priesthood office Enoch held? If so, how did he obtain it?

30. When a President of the Church dies, is the authority he held taken from the earth until another is appointed in his stead? If not, what happens to it in the meantime?

31. Is the President of the Church appointed by higher authority than that which he holds, by the same authority as that which he holds, or by lesser authority?

32. Can a lesser authority in the Priesthood appoint a higher authority?

33. What was taken out of Israel when Moses was translated?

34. Did Moses hold a self-perpetuating Priesthood office?

35. Who committed the Dispensation of the Gospel to the Savior?

36. In what priesthood capacity did Peter, James and John receive and hold the keys?

37. Were Peter, James and John equal in holding the keys, or did Peter hold them independently of James and John?

38. Do the keys restored by Peter, James and John comprehend all priesthood authority?

39. Does the office of President of the Church comprehend all priesthood authority?

40. What is the difference between that which was restored by Peter, James and John, and the office of President of the Church?

41. When Peter, James and John received the keys on the mount, did this detract from the priesthood authority held by Christ?

42. When the Twelve received the keys the spring before the Martyrdom at Carthage, did this detract from the authority of the Prophet Joseph?

43. Who was the Elias who appeared in the Kirtland Temple April 3, 1836?

44. Was the Elias spoken of in DC 110:12 the last one to hold the authority which he conferred, as mentioned in the preface to this section?

45. What authority was it that Elias conferred when he committed the dispensation of the Gospel of Abraham in the Kirtland Temple April 3, 1836?

46. Was the dispensation of the Gospel committed by Peter, James and John, or by Elias?

47. Was the authority conferred by Elias higher than that restored by Peter, James and John; was it the same, or was it lesser authority?

48. Who was the priest after the Order of Melchizedek and God's revelator to the human family after the Savior's Crucifixion?

49. What Priesthood authority remained upon the earth through John the Revelator?

50. How has the Kingdom of God remained set up from the days of Adam to the present time?

51. What is the Right of the Firstborn which was instituted before the earth, as spoken of in the Pearl of Great Price, Abr. 1:1-4?

52. What constitutes the Holy Apostleship?

53. What constitutes the Oracles of God?

54. Did Peter, James and John restore the authority mentioned in DC 132:7, that can be conferred upon only one man upon the earth at a time?

55. Was all presiding priesthood authority restored to the earth for the last time through the Prophet Joseph Smith?

56. What priesthood was hid from the world as mentioned in DC 86:8-11?

57. Did Joseph Smith hold the priesthood office Moses held? If so, when did he obtain it, who conferred this office upon him, and to whom did he give it?

58. Who is the Priest after the Order of Melchizedek today, and through what line did he receive his authority?

59. Who was the man who received the blessing that was to be put upon the head of the prophet Joseph Smith's posterity after him, as mentioned in DC '124:57?

60. Who is the promised seed of the prophet Joseph Smith, through whom the kindred of the earth are to be blessed?

APPENDIX III - On Ross and Joel

In the mid 1970's, I was totally done with Joel LeBaron's Church of the Firstborn of the Fullness of times. I did, however, have a large collection of their literature still stored at the house I was living in near San Diego, California. One day, a couple of people from Ross LeBaron's Church of the Firstborn came to see if they could get a few copies. They had been referred to me by someone in the CFBFT. No problem, take a few copies of each.

They asked me if I wanted to accompany them to Salt Lake City to meet their leader, Ross LeBaron. It had been many years since I had seen Ross, and I thought, "Why not?" But I wanted to take my wife Juleen with us. We then traveled to a place called Cane Beds, which is close to Colorado City in Arizona. Again, childhood memories that I wanted to share with my wife. Eventually, we arrived in Salt Lake, where they took me to meet Ross.

He was happy to see me again and, in a typical Ross manner, hired me and my wife to do some things. I was bending metal bars to insert into concrete and my wife was assembling jewelry to sell at the swap meet. Meanwhile, Ross is talking, preaching, and teaching.

What was important was that he didn't want my wife or any of my daughters. He didn't want my money, He didn't want anything except for me to pay attention to what he was trying to teach me. Mostly, the value of free agency and the need to seek our own revelations, make our own decisions, and be responsible for them.

I was ready to join him, but he didn't want me. What? He told me that I was part of his brother Joel's church and that it would be wrong to take me out of that group. I explained to him that I was already out and had no intention of going back. After a day or so, he decided that, yes, I could join his organization. Still no mention of tithing or other contributions.

Later, I was ordained by him as a Patriarch and told that I should work with the Mexican people. But not those that were in his brother's organization as they were part of Joel's organization. They could only be allowed into Ross' organization upon their sincere request. They could receive certain ordinances, but they were to be sealed to Joel.

My wife and I continued to work for him until we were ready to leave. Surprisingly, he paid us for all the work we had done. We thought we were just helping him out. We left still amazed that he didn't want anything from us. Not even our admiration or adoration. After that I was able to visit him many times and was never able to "gift" him with anything. I did buy him some recording equipment one time but before I left, he insisted on giving me equipment that far exceeded the value of what I had purchased for him.

Definitely not the typical church leader.

My work took me to Hawaii and later to the East Coast, so I did not get involved in the competition to be his successor. Several of his followers decided that they were his anointed and appointed successor. They apparently learned nothing from him and what he taught. All sought to become that "one man," aka Presiding Patriarch.

I eventually moved back to Baja California. I was past sixty-five and could now retire in Mexico. This allowed me to visit with my children often. One night, while I was staying with my daughter in Chula Vista, California, I woke up wide awake and heard one thing. "Joel came in the spirit of Elias. Ross came in the spirit of Elijah." I stayed awake the rest of the night digesting that. Yes, Joel had always said his priesthood came from Elias of DC 110. Yes, Ross had always traced his priesthood to the prophet Elijah of DC 110.

Could they have both been right? After much prayer and thought, I decided that the answer was yes. Different parts of what Joseph Smith established with his three different, independent groups. Ross with the church of the Father for exaltation. Joel restored the proper form of the church of the Son for salvation and a form of the church of the Holy Ghost for the rights of conscience.

At last, I understood what Joseph Smith had done and what the LeBarons were supposed to do.

www.ingramcontent.com/pod-product-compliance
Lightning Source LLC
Chambersburg PA
CBHW050106170426
43198CB00014B/2485